Poised for Greatness

How the Horse Became the Perfect Package of Strength, Speed, Courage and Beauty.

To Sarah

Thank you for helping Rose to be

Poised for Greatness

Mary Ann3

SPECIAL THANKS TO OUR TEAM

Mary Chris Foxworthy, Research Writer
Mary Chris' grandfather owned one of the last creameries in the United States that still used horse-drawn milk wagons. This sparked her life-long love affair with horses and passion for keeping horse history alive. After graduating from college with a degree in Food Science and Communications, Mary Chris bought her very first horse with her first paycheck. Since then, she has served on the board of various equine associations and held a judge's card in Carriage Driving. She is known for her work in the Gloria Austin Collection, and has published and presented numerous equine educational programs. She has written for several equine publications and won an award from American Horse Publications for one of her articles. Mary Chris is an active exhibitor in Carriage Driving and Dressage. Along with her husband, she enjoys spending time with their horses (two Morgans and a PRE), a bouncing Bearded Collie and two adult children and one grandchild.

BROUGHT TO YOU BY

The books created by Equine Heritage Institute are designed to preserve the history and majesty of the horse. Our goal is to find, understand, and pass on the valuable data about equine use and its influence on humanity. The Equine Heritage Institute is a not for profit 501(c)(3) and 100% of all proceeds from the sale of books, services, and products support Equine Heritage Institute's mission.

To make a donation to EHI, please visit EHI-store.square.site/s/shop

A COPY OF THE OFFICIAL REGISTRATION AND FINANCIAL INFORMATION MAY BE OBTAINED FROM THE DIVISION OF CONSUMER SERVICES BY CALLING TOLL-FREE WITHIN THE STATE REGISTRATION DOES NOT IMPLY ENDORSEMENT, APPROVAL, OR RECOMMENDATION BY THE STATE. s. 496.411, F.S.

1-800-HELP-FLA (435-7352)   www.FloridaConsumerHelp.com

The Horse

"We have had 6,000 years of history with the domesticated horse and only 100 years with the automobile."
Gloria Austin

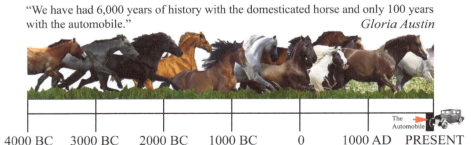

Poised For Greatness

First Publish 2022
Copyright © 2022 by Equine Heritage Institute, Inc.

Cover Artist, Juan Llamas
from Series Numeradas y Firmadas - 10 Caballos Españoles

All rights reserved. No part of this publication may be reproduced, distributed, or transmitted in any form or by any means, including photocopying, recording, or other electronic or mechanical methods, without the prior written permission of the publisher, except in the case of brief quotations embodied in critical reviews and certain other noncommercial uses permitted by copyright law. For permission requests, write to the publisher, addressed "Attention: Permissions Coordinator," at the address below.

Gloria Austin Carriage Collection, LLC; Equine Heritage Institute, Inc.
3024 Marion County Road Weirsdale, FL 32195
Office: (352) 753-2826 Fax: (352) 753-6186

Ordering Information: Quantity sales: Special discounts are available on quantity purchases by corporations, associations, and others. For details, contact the publisher at the address above.

ISBN: 978-1-951895-23-5

Table of Contents

- 9 Introduction
- 10 Chapter 1 ~ Evolution of the Horse
    - 12 The Dawn Horse ~ Eohippus
    - 15 Orohippus and Epihippus
    - 16 Mesohippus, Miohipus and Parahippus
    - 18 Toward the Modern Horse ~ Merychippus and Pliohippus
    - 20 Dinohippus
    - 21 Equus
    - 23 The Equine Family Today
- 24 Chapter 2 ~ Breeding Horses - Form to Function
    - 24 The Purpose of the Horse and Domestication
    - 35 Defining Form to Function
    - 38 Breeding Horses Through the Ages
        - 38 Natural Selection
        - 40 Natural Selection Transitions to Selective Breeding
        - 42 The First Horse Breeders - Creating Form to Function
        - 44 The Horses of Antiquity
            - 44 Misconceptions About Ancient Horses ~ Iberian, Barb and Arabian Horses
            - 47 Horses of the Steppes
            - 50 The Equids of the Sumerians 2600 - 2400 BC
            - 54 The Horses of the Ancient Greeks 1600 BC – 323 BC
            - 62 The Horses of the Hyksos 1600 BC
            - 63 The Horses of the Mitanni & Hittites 14th, 13th c. BC
            - 66 The Horses of the Kushites & Assyrians 8th & 7th c. BC
            - 70 The Horses of the Medes & Persians 1000 BC – 88 BC
            - 73 Horses in China 2nd Century BC
            - 75 Celtic Horses
            - 79 Roman Horses
            - 86 Review of Horse Types of Antiquity
        - 87 The Horses of the Middle Ages
            - 87 Monks and their Mounts
            - 88 Horses of the Knights
            - 89 Other Horses of the Middle Ages
        - 94 The Horses of the Age of Discovery 1350-1780
            - 95 Horses of the Ottoman Empire
            - 96 Horses of the Cossacks
            - 96 The Beginning of Horse Breeding in England
            - 99 The Thirty Years War and the Emergence of the Finnhorse

Table of Contents

- 100 France and the Breeding and Training of Horses
- 102 The Influence of Spanish Horses
- 103 Austria - The Hapsburgs and Horses
- 108 Horses Arrive in the Americas
- 110 The Breeding of Horses in Early America
- 113 Breeding Horses During the Industrial and Technical Revolutions 1750-1920
  - 114 Horses in The American Revolution
  - 115 Horses and the Expansion of the American West
  - 119 Horses in the American Civil War
  - 121 Horses and the Growth of Cities
  - 124 Horses in World War I
- 126 Breeding Horses in Modern Times
  - 126 On the Move Without Horses
  - 127 Purposeful Breeding in Modern Times
- 128 Chapter 3 ~ Understanding Purposeful Breeding in Modern Times
  - 128 Basic Equine Biomechanics
    - 129 The Equine Skeleton
    - 131 Beyond the Bones
    - 133 Basic Conformation Proportions
    - 138 Locomotion - Gaits of the Horse
    - 141 Other Gaits
    - 142 Understanding Conformation and Locomotion
  - 144 Analyzing Conformation for Function
    - 144 Jumping
    - 146 Dressage
      - 148 A word about collection
      - 149 A word about self-carriage
    - 150 Racing
    - 152 Harness Racing
    - 154 Endurance
    - 156 Saddle Seat
    - 158 Western Performance
    - 160 Trail/Packing
    - 162 Work Horses
    - 164 A Horse is a Horse
  - 165 Other considerations
- 170 Conclusion
  - 171 Sources and Further Reading

Gloria Austin's Collection of Books

www.GloriaAustin.com

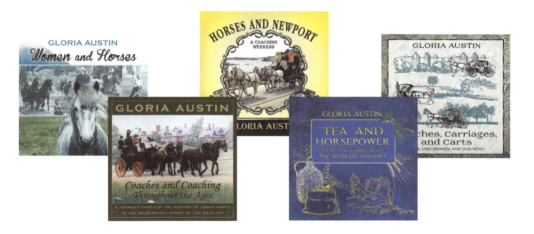

ENJOY OUR OTHER BOOKS

- Dance! To Improve Riding and Driving Your Horse
- The Brewster Story
- Carriage Lamps
- Gloria Austin's Carriage Collection
- A Glossary of Harness Parts
- Equine Elegance
- The Fire Horse
- Horse Basics 101
- The Unsung Heros of World War One
- The Horse, History, and Human Culture
- Horse Symbolism
- Horses of the Americas
- Horses and Newport
- The Mighty Mule
- Tea and Horsepower
- The Golden Carriage and the House of Hapsburg
- The American Horse
- Hold Your Horses, Horse Idioms and Other Sayings

Brought To You By The Equine Heritage Institute

Introduction

"A horse a horse! My kingdom for a horse!" This famous phrase originally occurred in Act-V, Scene-IV of William Shakespeare's play, *Richard III*. In the middle of a battle, King Richard's horse is killed and he wanders for hours trying to find it. Although used as a literary device, the phrase certainly captures the importance of the horse. From the trade routes to the battlefield to the farm to the show ring, horses have been an important part of human history for over six thousand years. In this age of cars and orbiting space stations, it's hard to think that a horse could be so important to human history. After all, how could an animal be smart enough or capable enough to be trained to be of such importance? Non horse owners are often amazed to find out that horses have distinct personalities and that they are capable of communicating with people. Research has proven that horses do not just 'behave' without considering the consequence of their actions. They are able to create a mental plan to evaluate how much a person is paying attention to them and to modify their communicative strategy accordingly; horses seem capable of creating a problem solving strategy. The horse has indeed then been a fitting partner for humans throughout history!

"Richard III, King of England, Uncle of Elizabeth of York, Great Uncle of Henry VIII" by lisby1 is marked with CC PDM [1]

The horse has impacted all sustainable cultures and civilizations around the world. The horse was the first thing which allowed man to travel faster then his two legs could carry him on land. The horse's size, power and speed offered man a distinct advantage in warfare, transportation, agriculture, commerce and industry. The horse has evolved into an animal that has the anatomy and physiology to do hard, laborious work and the horse's social abilities, as a herd animal with a hierarchical order, make the horse trainable by man.

Ashurbanipal II hunts wild asses, on a horseback. Alabaster-bas relief. From Room S, North Palace at Nineveh, Iraq, 645-635 BCE. British Museum, London. [3]

A gallic-roman harvester. Relief from Trier, a city on the banks of the Moselle in Germany. [2]

9

Chapter 1 - Evolution of the Horse

The evolution of the horse occurred over a geologic time scale of 55 million years, transforming the small, dog-sized, forest-dwelling Eohippus into the modern horse. Eohippus was for many years known as Hyracotherium, a subtle paleontological difference. Over the time of 55 million years, there have been a few hundred, now extinct, species of the genus Equus. Today there are only seven species of Equus. All horse breeds, from slim thoroughbred racehorses to stocky plow horses to tiny ponies, belong to a single species, Equus caballus.

The Eocene Epoch is a geological epoch that lasted from about 56 million to 33.9 million years ago. It is the second epoch of the Paleocene Period in the modern Cenozoic Era. The name Eocene comes from the Ancient Greek and refers to the "dawn" of modern ('new') fauna that appeared during the epoch. Over 55 million years ago horses were here on earth. Horses were here long before there were humans. Humans, in modern form, arrived during the Pleistocene Epoch. Humans have only been here about 200,000 years and civilization, as we know it, is only about 6,000 years old.

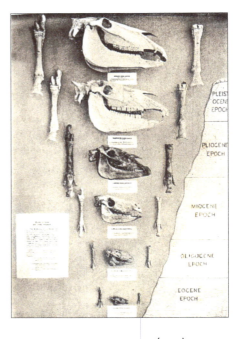

A series of skulls and feet. Eohippus, Mesohippus, Meryhippus, Hipparion and Equus. [4]

Through the study of fossils, paleontologists have found that horses originated, lived and evolved in North America and eventually migrated around the globe. The planet looked much different then. Millions of years ago horses were able to travel to Eurasia by crossing the Bering land bridge. Horses did not return to North America until they were brought by the explorers of the 1500s.

These two maps viewed from the North Pole at early and mid-Late Cretaceous, which illustrates the formation of Bering Land Bridge between Asia and North America. [5]

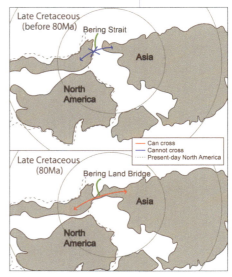

The evolutionary lineage of the horse is among the best documented in all paleontology. In recent years, the number of equid fossils has increased. The actual evolutionary progression from Eohippus to Equus has been discovered to be much more complex and multibranched than was initially supposed. Detailed fossil information on the rate and distribution of new equid species has also revealed that the progression between species was not as smooth and consistent as was once believed. The older version of the horse evolution was a single line. The newer version is a branching chain with several dead ends. It starts with the Hyracotherium (Eohippos the Dawn Horse) *(cited from: https://socratic.org/questions/what-is-the-correct-sequence-of-horse-evolution)*

Let's meet some of these ancestors of the modern horse.

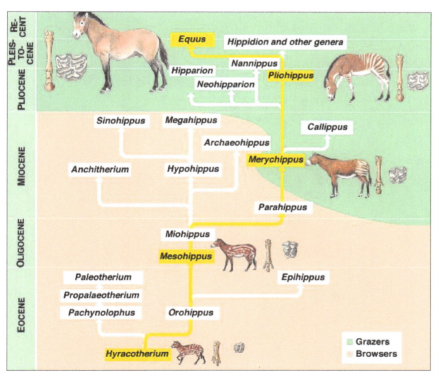

Modern View of Equid Evolution. Addison wesley Longman, Inc. [6]

The Dawn Horse - Eohippus

Paleontologists agree that the ancestor of all modern horses is **Eohippus,** the "dawn horse", a tiny (no more than 50 pounds), deer-like herbivore with four toes on its front feet and three toes on its back feet. Eohippus was, for many years, known as Hyracotherium.

Eohippus was a perissodactyl. The name is from the Greek perissos, "odd", and daktylos, "finger". A Perissodactyl is any member of a group of herbivorous mammals characterized by the possession of either one or three hoofed toes on each hind foot. They include horses, asses, zebras, tapirs and the rhinoceroses. The perissodactyls arose in the late Paleocene.

Fossils of the tiny pre-equines are rare. One of the most recent finds occurred in 2003 when fossil hunter Jim Tynsky found a fossil in the dried up bed of Fossil Lake near Kemmerer, Wyoming. The animal had four toes on the front feet and three on the back feet plus forty four teeth and a six-inch skull. The animal would have stood about twelve inches high. Experts agreed it truly was an early form of the horse from the Eocene period, 45 million to 55 million years ago. The fossil was moved to the Smithsonian in 2020.

Tynsky's find being prepped to transfer to the Smithsonian [7]

In the spring of 2015 the Eocene aged Green River Formation near Kemmerer, Wyoming yielded another amazing fossil discovery. A fully articulated primitive horse ancestor, since nicknamed "Olive", was found by brothers Mark and Mike Oliver.

"Olive" [8]

Eohippus

Eohippus is at least partly ancestral to all modern-day horses, as well as to the numerous species of prehistoric horse, such as Epihippus and Merychippus, that roamed the North American and Eurasian plains millions of years ago. The multi toed ancestor of today's horse was very fast in order to evade predators. As with many such evolutionary precursors, Eohippus did not look much like a horse, with its slender, deer-like, 50-pound body and three and four-toed feet. Judging by the shape of its teeth, Eohippus munched on low-lying leaves rather than grass. In the early Eocene epoch, during which Eohippus lived, grasses had yet to spread across the North American plains, which spurred the evolution of grass-eating equids. Eohippus put most of its weight on a single toe of each foot, anticipating later equine developments.

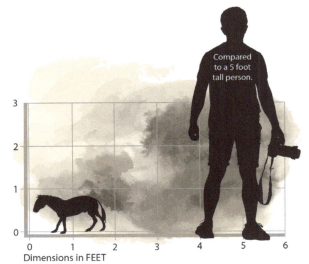

Eohippus at 30 centimetres high (.98 feet) at shoulder. [9]

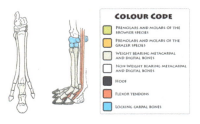

Eohippus leg [9]

Although Eohippus fossils occur in both the Old and the New World, the subsequent evolution of the horse took place chiefly in North America. *(cited from: https://paleontologyworld.com/exploring-prehistoric-life/evolution-horse and https://www.britannica.com/animal/perissodactyl and https://www.thoughtco.com/eohippus-dawn-horse-1093222)*

Orohippus and Epihippus

During the remainder of the Eocene epoch, evolutionary changes were mostly in dentition. **Orohippus**, a genus from the middle Eocene, and **Epihippus,** a genus from the late Eocene, resembled Eohippus in size and in the structure of the limbs. But the form of the cheek teeth—the four premolars and the three molars found in each half of both jaws—had changed somewhat. In Eohippus the premolars and molars were clearly distinct, the molars being larger. In Orohippus the fourth premolar had become similar to the molars, and in Epihippus both the third and fourth premolars had become molar-like. In addition, the individual cusps that characterized the cheek teeth of Eohippus had given way in Epihippus to a system of continuous crests or ridges running the length of the molars and molariform premolars.

Orohippus, 1.9 feet high at the shoulder. [9]

Although still a primitive horse, the teeth of Epihippus and Orohippus show a trend more towards the grinding of grasses over the slicing of plant vegetation like leaves. This is a reaction to the changing ecosystems of the Eocene which saw the beginning of a reduction in forests with their subsequent replacement by grassy plains. This process would go on throughout the forthcoming Oligocene and Miocene epochs, steadily driving horses towards the modern forms we know today. These changes, which represented adaptations to a more-specialized browsing diet, were retained by all subsequent ancestors of the modern horse.

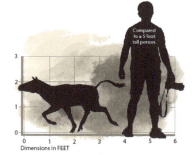

Epihippus, 1.9 feet high at the shoulder. [9]

Orohippus was slightly larger than Eohippus but shared its generally primitive post-cranial skeletal structure. For example, as in humans, the lower limb bones of the forelimb, the radius and ulna, of Eohippus and Orohippus are distinct and unfused. This is the primitive condition for mammals, and permits rotational movement at the elbow and wrist joints. This condition is retained by animals such as small forest dwellers who must maneuver over uneven terrain. Orohippus also differs from Eohippus by having more enlarged middle digits on its fore and hind feet, and by displaying a complete loss of the first and fifth (thumb and pinkie) toes of the hindlimb.

(cited from: http://www.prehistoric-wildlife.com/species/e/epihippus.html and https://www.floridamuseum.ufl.edu/fossil-horses/gallery/orohippus/)

Mesohippus, Miohippus and Parahippus

Like many fossil horses, **Mesohippus** was common in North America. Mesohippus had longer legs than its predecessor, Eohippus. Mesohippus stood about 60 cm (23.6 in or 6 hands) tall. This equid is the first fully tridactyl horse in the evolutionary record, with the third digit being longer and larger than its second and fourth digits. Mesohippus had not developed a hoof at this point, rather it still had pads. The face of Mesohippus was longer and larger than earlier equids. It had a slight facial fossa, or depression, in the skull. The eyes were rounder, and were set wider apart and farther back. Unlike earlier horses, its teeth were low crowned and contained a single gap behind the front teeth, where the bit now rests in the modern horse. In addition, it had another grinding tooth, making a total of six. Mesohippus was a browser that fed on tender twigs and fruit. The cerebral hemisphere, or cranial cavity, was notably larger than that of its predecessor; its brain was similar to that of modern horses. *(cited from: https://en.wikipedia.org/wiki/Mesohippus)*

Mesohippus, 1.9 feet high at the shoulder. [9]

Miohippus was one of the most successful prehistoric horses. This three-toed genus was represented by about a dozen different species, all of them indigenous to North America from about 35 to 25 million years ago. The genus itself consisted of two basic types, one adapted for life on prairies and the other best suited to forests and woodlands. It was the prairie variety that led to Equus. The woodland version, with its elongated second and fourth toes, spawned small descendants that went extinct in Eurasia at the cusp of the Pliocene epoch, about five million years ago. Miohippus was a bit larger than Mesohippus (about 100 pounds for a full-grown adult, compared to 50 or 75 pounds). It had a slightly

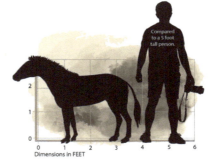

Miohippus, 2.5 feet high at the shoulder. [9]

Miohippus skull [9]

longer skull. Its facial fossa was deeper and more expanded, and the ankle joint was subtly different. Miohippus also had a variable extra crest on its upper molars, which gave it a larger surface area for chewing tougher forage. This would become a typical characteristic of the teeth of later equine species. *(cited from: https://www.thoughtco.com/miohippus-miocene-horse-1093245 and https://fossil.fandom.com/wiki/Miohippus)*

Parahippus was larger than Miohippus, with longer legs and face. The bones in the legs were fused and this, along with muscle development, allowed Parahippus to move with forward-and-back strides. Flexible leg rotation was eliminated, so that the animal was better adapted to fast forward running on open ground without moving from side to side. Most importantly, Parahippus was able to stand on its middle toe, instead of walking on pads, which gave it the ability to run faster; its weight was supported by ligaments under the fetlock to the big central toe. The side toes were almost vestigial, and seldom touched the ground. Since leafy food had become scarce, these animals were forced to subsist on the newly evolved grasses that were by now taking over the plains, and their teeth adapted accordingly. The extra molar crest that was variable in Miohippus became permanent in Parahippus. The molars developed high crowns and a hard covering for grinding the grass, which was typically covered with high-silica dust and sand. *(cited from: https://en.wikipedia.org/wiki/Parahippus)*

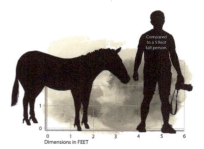

Parahippus, 3.2 feet high at the shoulder. [9]

Toward the Modern Horse Merychippus

Merychippus was something of a watershed in equine evolution: this was the first prehistoric horse to bear a marked resemblance to modern horses. The tooth pattern in Merychippus is basically the same as that in the modern horse; the teeth became higher and dental cement appeared, which allowed a grazing mode of life. Other developments in the skeleton are also evident: its size increased so that Merychippus was almost as large as a modern pony and the skull became more elongated in a very horselike fashion. The limbs as well became more horselike in proportion and better adapted to running. In some forms the three toes remained comparatively large, but in progressive species of Merychippus the two side toes were short and small. The center toe was much larger than the others and carried most of the animal's weight. A well-developed hoof was present on the large central toe. *(cited from: https://www.thoughtco.com/merychippus-ruminant-horse-1093241 and https://www.britannica.com/animal/Merychippus)*

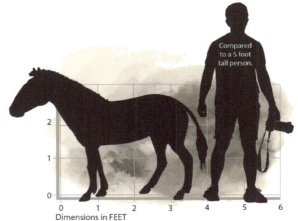

Merychippus, 3.2 feet high at the shoulder. [9]

Merychippus skull and leg [9]

18

Pliohippus

Pliohippus lived about 12 million years ago in North America. It had evolved into the first one-toed horse, and the two side toes had been reduced to splint bones. As a result, it was the forerunner of the modern day horse. This became an endpoint branch as it died out in the Pliocene. It developed from Merychippus of the Miocene period. It was a grazing animal in North America with high-crowned teeth and in turn it gave rise to Dinohippus which in turn evolved into Equus, the modern horse. Its skull had a depression in the skull, called the pre-orbital depression, located in front of the eyes and the function of this is not really known. Some have suggested it was for the attachment for specialized lip muscles, but others have suggested this depression may have played a role in vocalizations. *(cited from: https://www.equineguelph.ca/equimania/DomesticationTimeline/pliohippus.html)*

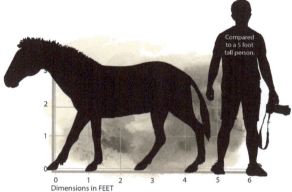

Pliohippus - Roughly about 3.9 feet tall at the shoulder, but some variance between species. [9]

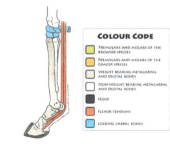

Pliohippus skull and leg [9]

Dinohippus

Dinohippus is believed to be the last direct ancestor of Equus, the family that includes today's horses, asses and zebras. It was a grazing animal in North America about 13-5 million years ago. This species had a shallow depression in the skull in front of its eyes. The function is not known but it could have been for muscle attachment or some have suggested it could be the location of glands.

Dinohippus - Roughly about 4.9 feet tall at the shoulder, but some variance between species. [9]

Dinohippus is the first horse that shows evidence of the passive "stay apparatus" an anatomical feature that is well-formed in Equus. The stay apparatus is an important "safety" feature as it helped the horse to stand for long periods of time with less energy use. So, this was one of the first horses that could sleep while standing.

An interesting feature of Dinohippus is that there was a variation in the numbers for toes in this group. Some fossils in Nebraska had three toes, but in other areas individuals had one toe. *(cited from: https://equineguelph.ca/learn_objects/evolutiontimeline/dinohippus.html)*

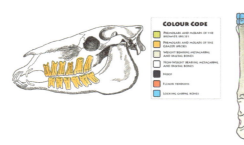  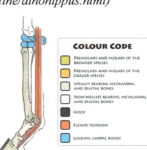

Dinohippus skull and leg [9]

20

Equus

The Pleistocene epoch was 1.6 million years ago to 10,000 years ago. This is the period when **Equus** appeared. The modern day species of Equus (horses, zebras, and asses) have been around for about two million years. They are very different from the earliest known horse, Hyracotherium, otherwise known as "Dawn Horse".

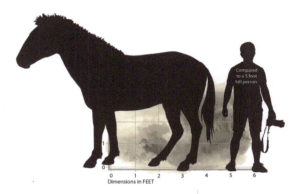

The period is popularly known as the Ice Age, although the name is somewhat misleading. We know that huge sheets of ice covered much of the earth during the Pleistocene epoch. But modern geologists believe that glaciers occupied only small areas of the earth at any one time.

Equus - Roughly about 4.7 feet tall at the shoulder, but some variance between species. [9]

They would form in different places at different times, advance, and then gradually melt and recede. During the glacial stages, temperatures would drop on average 5 to 7 degrees Celcius (9 to 13 degrees Fahrenheit). In between, the "interglacial stages" had temperatures similar to, or slightly above, our current climates.

But even these slight, average differences had huge impacts on the animals living through the period. The ice changed the surface of the earth and helped provide a suitable climate for huge Ice Age mammals, such as the mastodon and saber-tooth tiger, to thrive. Equus, the "modern horse" species, developed. The first true humans appeared during the Pleistocene epoch. In fact, early humans have left us drawings and cave paintings of their neighbors: mastodons, woolly mammoths, bears, rhinoceros, tigers and horses. Toward the end of the epoch, the glaciers receded, the climate changed again and the huge mammals disappeared from the fossil record. Man continued to evolve and adapt and recent theories suggest that, along with long reproduction cycles, humans hunting these mammals contributed to their extinction.

It was also during this period (about 8000 BC) that horses died out on the North American continent. The vast grasslands that nurtured early horse species had been covered with ice. New predators, including humans, challenged the horses and the species disappeared from North America for thousands of years. Meanwhile, across the sea, horses were becoming a fixture of many ancient civilizations. The horse was domesticated about 6000 years ago and used for transportation and travel, allowing humans to range much further away than they could ever do on foot. Due to this travel, domestication of the horse was widespread throughout Asia, North Africa, and Europe about 5000 years ago and played an important role in warfare, along with its role for transportation and draft work. It was not until Columbus' voyage of 1492 that the horse was brought back to the Americas. Soon after, large numbers of horses were sent over in ships to the settlements and horses once again ran in herds in the Great Plains of North America, in the same area where the evolution of the horse had originated 55 to 58 million years earlier.
(cited from: http://netnebraska.org/basic-page/television/wild-horses-evolution)

Equus had one toe and the two side toes had developed into the two side bones on each leg that we know today as splints. The genus of all modern equines, the first Equus was about 13.2 hands tall, pony size, with a classic "horsey" body – rigid spine, long neck, legs and nose and fused leg bones with no rotation. The brain was a bit larger than Dinohippus. Equus was (and still is) one-toed, with side ligaments that prevent twisting of the hoof. This species has high-crowned, straight, grazing teeth with strong crests. It was a grazing animal, living on grasses in open areas. Its last ancestor was Dinohippus. The equine family is the only single-toed animal today. The family today includes horses, asses and zebras. With the exception of Australia and Antarctica, Equus fossils have been found on every continent.*(cited from: https://www.equineguelph.ca/equimania/DomesticationTimeline/equus.html)*

Equus skull and leg [9]

The Equine Family Today

Horses, zebras, and asses constitute the family Equidae. All of the modern members of the family are placed in the genus Equus. *(cited from: https://www.britannica.com/topic/list-of-horses-zebras-and-asses-2058537*

DOMESTIC HORSES AND RELATIVES
64 chromosomes

Some breeds of horse (Equus caballus)

- American Quarter Horse
- American Saddlebred
- Arabian horse
- Barb
- Belgian horse
- Cayuse
- Cleveland Bay
- Clydesdale
- Criollo
- Hackney
- Lipizzaner
- Missouri fox-trotting horse
- Morgan
- Percheron
- Shire
- Standardbred
- Suffolk
- Tennessee walking horse
- Thoroughbred

Some color types and color breeds

- Albino
- Appaloosa
- Palomino
- Pinto

Some breeds of pony (Equus caballus)

- Connemara
- Dartmoor
- Hackney pony
- Pony of the Americas
- Shetland pony
- Welsh pony

Asses (Equus asinus)
- donkey (E. asinus) 62 chromosomes
    - hinny (E. asinus × E. caballus)
    - mule (E. asinus × E. caballus) 63 chromosomes

WILD EQUINES

Asses
- African wild ass (E. africanus
- kiang (E. kiang)
- onager (E. onager)

Horses
- Przewalski's horse (subspecies E. caballus prze walskii or E. ferus przewalskii) 66 chromosomes
- tarpan (subspecies E. caballus caballus; recently extinct)

Zebra 44 – 62 chromosomes (depending on species)
- Grevy's zebra (E. grevyi)
- mountain zebra (E. zebra)
- plains zebra (E. quagga)

Chapter 2 - Breeding Horses - Form to Function

The Purpose of the Horse and Domestication

As we learned in Chapter 1, horses evolved as the environment changed; their form changed and adapted to the environment. The theory of evolution by natural selection, first formulated in Darwin's book "On the Origin of Species" in 1859, is the process by which organisms change over time as a result of changes in physical or behavioral traits. Since the horse is a prey animal, those that could run the fastest survived. Those that had locking patella's and could sleep standing up to get away quicker survived. Those that had eyes on the sides of their head to see approaching danger, survived. Those that had better hearing and smell for approaching danger survived; and those who's digestive system allowed it to eat and run, survived. Through natural selection (selecting mates in the wild) the horse evolved into the fast and strong animal that we know today. Once humans came on the scene, the horse became functional; that is, it served a purpose for the humans. Over time that purpose changed and thus the form of the horse changed as well.

Even though the horse was on earth long before humans, it was not the first animal domesticated by humans. The following is a list of animals and the approximate millennium and location in which they were domesticated:

- Dog 12000 BC (Eurasia)
- Sheep 9000 BC (Iraq)
- Goat 7000 BC (Turkey)
- Swine 7000 BC (Turkey)
- Cattle 6500 BC (Greece)
- Reindeer 5000 BC (Scandinavia)
- Horse 4000 BC (Kazakhstan)

Approximate Time Frame of Domestication Based on Archaeology [10]

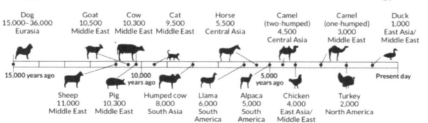

The horse was domesticated rather late because of the very factors that made it useful; its speed and endurance made it difficult to catch. Catching the horse and keeping it from running away when frightened was a real challenge for early man. Smaller animals were easier to tame and tether. Even today's domestic horses in a pasture are sometimes difficult to catch. The gaits of the horse range from four miles per hour to fifty five miles per hour.

The horse's size and speed made it significant. It had the ability to carry and pull weight. Its anatomy, with sturdy hooves and a unique digestive system, allowed it to eat and run. Its social ability with hierarchal and herding instincts allowed man to more easily give it direction.

Throughout history the horse has been used for many purposes.

- Food
- Herding
- Warfare
- Transportation
- Communication
- Agriculture
- Trade
- Commerce
- Pleasure
- Sport
- Religion
- Symbol
- Status
- Gifts
- Art
- Industry
- Competition
- Recreation

Emperor Caligula on horseback Caligvla. Roman emperors on horseback. Imperatorvm XII. New Hollstein Dutch 1182 [11]

When humans first encountered horses, they hunted them and used them for food. It never occurred to them to domesticate the horse. There is no written documentation to determine if horses were ridden or driven first; we can only imagine some daring person decided that getting on a horse or hooking a horse to something to pull might be a good idea. Archaeologist Melinda Zeder, from the Smithsonian Institution in Washington, D.C., says, "Horses caused the first globalization. They allowed cultures to grow from isolated pockets to interconnected spheres of influence."

Image of a horse from the Lascaux caves made by the Cro-Magnon peoples at their hunting route in the Stone age. [12]

Archaeologists have found more than one hundred caves in Europe with paintings of at least four thousand animals. Nearly one third of the animals in painted caves are paintings of horses. Almost all of the caves are in southern France and northern Spain. One cave in France, called Chauvet Cave, has been dated to at least 32,000 years ago. Other caves in Lascaux, France and Altamira, Spain are about 15,000 years old.

The domestication of all animals was a process rather than an event and it occurred slowly over a period of thousands of years in different regions of the world. At the early point in human history, there is no evidence that humans thought about domesticating horses by riding horses or driving horses but the cave paintings show that humans were very familiar with horses. Most of these developments occurred before writing was invented so we depend on archaeological evidence to help us understand what happened. The DNA of domestic horses is very diverse. This suggests they may have been domesticated in more than one place, from several different wild horse populations.

Archaeological evidence tells us that horses were domesticated in the middle Holocene era, a period roughly from 7,000 to 5,000 years ago. Archaeologists have found horse manure in the post holes of what might have been a stable built around 5000 BC in what is now Kazakhstan. Since early humans were nomads, that meant that they moved to places where they could find food and water. One of the ways they moved was by following herds of horses. While the horse still remained a "wild animal", humans and horses grew closer together. Humans could attract the horse by providing food and providing shelter. Early humans found that they could milk the lactating mares and serve the milk to their own families. The nomads' trade was not based on gain but rather on providing themselves with goods they did not produce. Horses were crucial to the life of the nomads; not only were they essential for their nomadic lifestyle but also used as trade for goods they could not hunt or forage.

Humans, in modern form, arrived during the Pleistocene Epoch. The Paleolithic Age, or "Old Stone" Culture, existed during the Pleistocene Epoch. It covers about 99% of the time period of human technological prehistory. It extends from the earliest known use of stone tools, about 3.3 million years ago, to the end of the Pleistocene Epoch. Between 2.6 and 2.5 million years ago, the earth got significantly hotter and drier. Before that climate shift, our distant human ancestors were subsisting mostly on fruits, leaves, seeds, flowers, bark and tubers. As the temperature rose, the lush forests shrank and great grasslands thrived. As green plants became scarcer, evolutionary pressure forced early humans to find new sources of energy. The grassland savannas supported growing numbers of grazing herbivores.

The Paleolithic Age is characterized with the production of tools and weapons by hewing or carving. Archaeologists have found large herbivore bones dating from 2.5 million years ago with telltale cut marks from crude stone tools. Most of the tools that were made at the time were used for hunting, animal skin peeling and cutting of the animal meat. Such tools were rough and imperfect.

Chase Hunt [13]

Our ancient ancestors weren't capable hunters yet; they likely scavenged the meat from fallen carcasses. Early humans lived in groups and traveled extensively in search of food and shelter. Entire human communities depended on successful hunting to survive. Eventually humans became proficient hunters. Fossils of antelopes, zebras and similar animals were found alongside the early human fossils and stone tools in the 1.8-million-year old deposits. Paleolithic people most often used the so-called "chase hunt". They hunted herd type animals and used trickery instead of offensive weapons. Chase hunts forced animals into the mud and the straits, where they had no way out, then they would chase them towards steep ravines where animals would fall and break legs or die. The "hunters" secured themselves with meat, fat, bones, hair, horns and skin; thus they attained everything that was of great importance in their fight for life. The first shelters that Paleolithic people built were near water where animals would come to drink; it was the easiest place to find prey.

Head-Smashed-In Buffalo Jump, World Heritage Site in the foothills of the Rocky Mountains, Alberta, Canada. [14]

Transporting the food that was found was most likely accomplished by dragging it. Eventually humans discovered how to use rope to aid in dragging. Our ancestors depended on the use of rope for many reasons. Rope and twine were critical components in the technology of mobile hunters and gatherers. It is probable that the earliest "ropes" were naturally occurring lengths of plant fiber, such as vines, followed soon by the first attempts at twisting and braiding these strands together to form the first proper ropes in the modern sense of the word. An ancient rope tool, made from mammoth ivory, was discovered in Hohle Fels Cave in Germany. The ancient rope tool is unique as it underlines the importance of fiber technology and the importance of rope and

Rope making tool from mammoth ivory from Hohle Fels Cave in southwestern Germany, ca. 40,000 years old. Image credit: University of Tübingen. [15]

string for mobile hunters and gatherers. The first known rope and twine dates back to about 26000 BC. Although this early rope and twine no longer exists, it left impressions in fired clay. Fragments of two-ply laid rope of about 7 mm diameter from 15000 BC were found fossilized in a cave at Lascaux, France. Hemp was often used for making rope. Hemp cloth from approximately 8000 BC was found at Catal Hüyük (in Anatolia, in modern day Turkey).

The Neolithic Revolution, also called the Agricultural Revolution, marked the transition in human history from small, nomadic bands of hunter-gatherers to larger, agricultural settlements and early civilization. The Neolithic Age is sometimes called the New Stone Age. The Neolithic Revolution started around 10000 BC in the Fertile Crescent, a boomerang-shaped region of the Middle East where humans first took up farming. Shortly after, Stone Age humans in other parts of the world also began to practice agriculture, develop more advanced tools and make pottery. Civilizations and cities grew out of the innovations of the Neolithic Revolution. The earth entered a warming trend around 14,000 years ago at the end of the last Ice Age. Some scientists theorize that climate changes drove the Agricultural Revolution. Other scientists suggest that intellectual advances in the human brain may have caused people to settle down. Religious artifacts and artistic imagery—progenitors of human civilization—have been uncovered at the earliest Neolithic settlements.

The first livestock were domesticated from animals that Neolithic humans hunted for meat. The first farm animals included pigs, goats, sheep and cattle. These originated in Mesopotamia between 10,000 and 13,000 years ago. Water buffalo and yak were domesticated shortly after in China, India and Tibet. Reindeer were one of the first animals to pull loads. Draft animals including oxen, donkeys and camels appeared much later—around 4000 BC. Many of the villages began to use

Neolithic Village [16]

horses for food and milk. They built herds like they did with their other animals. These villages created trading agreements with other sedentary villages and with many nomadic tribes. Periodically nomadic tribes would raid villages and they would adapt and develop defensive measures.

Skara Brae Neolithic Village, Stromness, Orkney Islands [17]

Between 3900 BC and 3000 BC the Piora Oscillation (a shift in weather patterns toward colder and wetter weather) occurred. Colder weather is not good for most fodder crops. As crops failed and weather grew colder, agriculture began to fail. The pastoral lifestyle of traveling with herds to known good feeding grounds failed as the climate shifted. Piora Oscillation is also associated with a sudden onset of drier weather in the central Sahara, shifting it to the desert it is today. This change in climate caused the horse to become valuable in other ways. The horse could handle the cold, clear the ground to get to plants under the snow and digest low quality fodder without problems. To this day, nomadic tribes in the steppes use the horse to break the crusted snow and ice and allow other grazers to follow them and access the cleared ground to eat.

In some of the earliest cave drawings ever found, the mighty horse reigns supreme over all other animals. Depicted with precision and gusto, this majestic creature is hard to miss. These images were drawn thousands of years before humans started riding horses. Georges Sauvet, an expert in prehistoric art, has collected more than 4,700 examples of Palaeolithic drawings, paintings and engravings anywhere from 12,000 to 30,000 years old, originating in what is today France and Spain. The horse is the preferred subject. One of the give-aways, he argues, is the direction the horses are facing. While most animals are drawn oriented to the left, horses are the only species that is predominantly oriented to the right. It's obvious that horses meant something special to early humans but exactly what, no one can say for sure. Perhaps it was the elusiveness of the horse that made them seem so special. Perhaps it was the desire to harness the majesty and power of the horse. Herding horses was difficult. Horses could travel great distances at speed and were not subject to any controls other than the lead horse. A tribe might spend days finding the herd and rounding them up. The solution seemed simple, begin to ride the horse and use it to guide the herd. While the concept seemed simple, the execution might have taken hundreds of years to implement.

Since people only walked or traveled by rivers, it limited where they could go. They did not meet people from other lands that did not live near the river that flowed near their city and they did not learn about all the discoveries and inventions made by other people. People in China, people in India, people in Egypt and people in Europe did not know much about each other. Each culture was discovering things not knowing what the other one was doing or discovering. But one thing all peoples were doing almost everywhere was figuring out how to partner with the horse. There is still debate over the first use of the horse and where that occurred. Evidence of bit wear has been found at Dereivka from around 4000 BC which would pre-date the introduction of the wheel and thus indicate that riding may have occurred before driving. Initial use of the horse probably differed from culture to culture as they came to utilize the horse depending on:

Chariot drawn by bulls or steers, clay rhyton. Karfi, Crete, Late postpalatial period (LM IIIC), 1100-1000 BC. Archaeological Museum of Heraklion. [18]

- If they had the wheel
- If they had previous experience in driving animals
- Type of lifestyle - did they need to use the horse as a draft animal and did their stage of development have the technology in place to harness a horse to a vehicle.

Early primitive man came to realize that rolling a load was much easier than dragging. Most inventions were actually inspired by the natural world. One of the reasons it took a long time for man to invent the wheel is because there was no organic example of the wheel in nature. The earliest depiction of a wheeled vehicle is from c 3000 BC by a scribe at Uruk, a Sumerian city-state of the early Bronze Age era. It shows the combination of a sledge with that of a sledge on wheels. It adds to the theory that the wheeled vehicle

Clay chariot model, beginning of the 2nd millennium BC, Musée du Louvre [19]

31

developed from the addition of wheels to the already established sledge.

The "Standard of Ur" is the earliest depiction of equines in draft. It is on a trapezoidal box (about 9.5" long, 8.5" high) which may have been used as a standard (a box carried on a pole for ceremonies). The Standard pictures animals on the panels and depicts War and Peace. It is dated 2600 BC from the region of Mesopotamia. It is currently housed in the British Museum and was originally found in a burial site at Ur in modern day Iraq. The Battle Cars on the Standard of Ur had four two-piece wheels and were pulled by three or four Onagers. Control was obtained by a single rein (jerk line) attached to a nose ring which was what had been used with bovine. They used pairs with a single yoke and neck and girth system of harnessing. This type of harness was impractical for horses due to the weight of the vehicle and the yoke. The neck strap would have pushed against the horse's windpipe.

The Standard of Ur [20]

Kikkuli text. Clay tablet, a training program for chariot horses 14th century BC.[21]

The first known written information about horses was in 1345 BC. In 1345 BC a Mitannian horse-master known as Kikkuli wrote the Chariot Training Manual. It gave a detailed plan for training and caring for horses. He developed a new method of training called "interval training". The horse would pace a league (about 3.5 miles) then run a furlong (about 220 yards.) After that, the horse would rest and then more exercise. Each few days the horse was asked to do more than the day before and rest and feed were increased as needed. There were always many baths included too. Interval training is still used today to strengthen the horse's muscles and respiratory system. Even human athletes do interval training.

The horse came to be a valuable military asset - no longer just a food source of the nomads. Horse breeding became very important. Kingdoms and powerful rulers aspired to have large stables to supply their armies with horses for their chariots.

The horse and chariot served as a catalyst for economic, political and social change, and the development of the ancient world. According to John Keegan, in *The History of Warfare,* men were driving chariots into battle for about 1,000 years before riding to war on the backs of horses. The horse and chariot allowed kingdoms to become empires. The noble horse and chariot were so revered that they were even depicted in the heavens. The horse was the first thing that allowed man to go faster than his two legs could carry him on land. The horse increased human traveling speed ten times over the use of the ox and mule and, even more important, the horse was impressive and intimidating with its spirited attitude.

Horses in ancient times were much smaller than most horses are today. Most horses were only about 12 to13 hands high. The average horse now is 15 to 16 hands high. Horses were, and still are, measured by how many hands high they are from the ground to the withers. One of the oldest units of length measurement used in the ancient world was the 'cubit' which was the length of the arm from the tip of the finger to the elbow. This could then be subdivided into shorter units like the foot, hand (which at 4 inches is still used today for expressing the height of horses) or some units were added together to make longer units like the pace.

The horse was indeed "**Poised for Greatness**"! Anatomically and physiologically the horse had evolved to become a partner for humans. The horse was no longer a food source. The horse had size, speed and the ability to carry weight as well as pull weight. Horses are amazingly communicative and thrive in social settings. These qualities are part of the reason why horses can develop such a strong bond

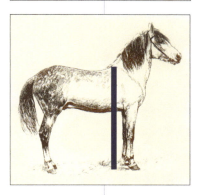

Ancient Measures [22]

with humans. Horses command respect in many ways, especially with their stature. They are massive beings, with enough brain and brawn to intimidate people. However, they can trust and will allow people to approach them. In both human dynamics and horse herds, there is a hierarchy structure. Whether it's in families or employment, people are consistently operating within a hierarchy. Horses also have a similar family structure as humans, where male and female horses stick together and their offspring leave the nest once they're mature. Horses are also communicative and expressive, much like people. They can display different attitudes and emotions, which makes them relatable to humans. *(cited from: https://agapepetservices.com/make-horse-human-relationships-unique/)*

Defining Form to Function

The definition of conformation can be articulated in different ways. Websters defines conformation as: "form or outline of an animal". A more accurate definition is: "the relationship of form and function". This defines the way that the horse's structure allows it to perform its method of ambulation either on its own or while working or performing for man. Cardiovascular, respiratory, nervous and digestive systems also contribute to how well a horse can perform. The horse also has a unique quality to give maximum effort when asked. In addition, there are numerous extrinsic factors that affect a horse's performance such as the degree of training, physical fitness, state of health, shoeing, tack used and certainly, the rider or driver. However, form is of primary interest when it comes to function. Bacteriologist Szent-Gyorgyi in 1950 said, when describing a single cell, that "there is no real difference between structure and function; they are two sides of the same coin. If a structure does not tell us about function it means we have not looked at it correctly." This statement adds succinct evidence as to why conformation of the horse should be evaluated as it relates to the function.

For centuries, much of a horse's success or failure has been attributed to its conformation. There are sketches and descriptions of Alexander the Great's horse Bucephalus (356 –323 BC) and Xenophon (430 –354 BC) goes into detail about good and bad conformation.

Statue group of Alexander & Bucephalus, 1704. [23]

Type of horse also plays a role in the success of a horse's function. The difference in horse types is exemplified by the extremes of the miniature horse and the large draft horse. Type is defined as the inherited characteristics of an animal that fit it for a certain use. For example, the Thoroughbred type is suited to running. The American Quarter Horse type is designed to perform activities that require quick speed and muscle mass. The Arabian type is suited to travel great distances with the least amount of expended energy. Within each type of horse, there is a standard of excellence based upon abilities. In an evaluation of the horse's conformation relevant to the type, it becomes obvious that one horse cannot do all the tasks that man asks of them. Regardless, correct conformation is fundamental in any type of horse. The head and neck position, the angle of the shoulder and the angle of the croup are three of the most significant factors that determine the standard of excellence of a horse within its type. In fact, these factors also assist in defining the type of horse.

The gaits of the horse contribute to their dynamics of locomotion and conformation is basic as to how the horse ambulates. The dynamics of locomotion are the result of synchronization of the actions of the horse's biological systems. The skeleton is the key to a horse's method of progression and the foundation of its conformation. Most lameness is the direct effect of stress, strain and concussion on the musculoskeletal system; therefore, conformation defects that enhance these forces are the most significant and provide a basis to establish what value should be assigned to the various conformation defects. Therefore, conformation becomes the common denominator to the horse's ability to perform and stay sound.

Richard Stone Reeves is considered to be the 20th century's premier racing portraitist and perhaps the most important American painter of sporting art ever. Known for his accuracy and realism, Reeves' ability to capture the personality and character of each subject was legendary. In 1970, Reeves, was commissioned by the Thoroughbred Record magazine to paint "The Perfect Horse". In this work; the artist used Tie Polleto's head and neck, Citation's shoulder, Jay Trump's forelegs, Vaguely Nobel's middle piece, Buck Passer's quarters and hindlimbs, and Graustark's color. In his description of "The Perfect Horse," he stated that "all the horses were top class runners indeed; there is hardly a top class runner in existence with faulty conformation. [24]

The correlation of the three factors (standard of excellence, dynamics of locomotion, and soundness) provides a method to better understand the meaning of the conformation relationship of form to function. More and more objective evaluations of conformation are being developed with the advent of sophisticated research enhanced by the application of modalities. These modalities provide specific information as to the movement of the horse and define the effects of conformation on the movement of specific parts of the horse. *(cited from: https://aaep.org/sites/default/files/issues/proceedings-08proceedings-z9100108000001.PDF)*

Confirmation is inherited— good and bad. Through the centuries, as the function (purpose) of the horse changed, so did the form (conformation). For thousands of years the horse evolved based upon survival of the fittest. Once domesticated, the conformation of the horse was influenced through selective breeding by humans based upon the functional needs.

Breeding Horses Through the Ages

Natural Selection

Over millions of years primitive horses migrated from North American across the Bering land-bridge. The last representatives of the genus Equus mysteriously died out on North America about 10,000 years ago and did not return to the Americas until the 1500s. Horses did spread out over Asia, Europe and Africa though and evolved into the familiar shapes of the present-day zebras, donkeys and horses.

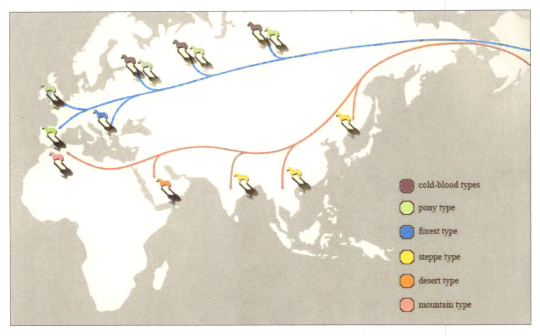

Migratory paths of prehistoric horses from North America to Asia, Europe and Africa. Different geographical breeds or subspecies of horse evolved wherever individual populations were isolated for long periods of time. The map is partly conjecture but by and large it is based on authenticated finds. [25]

In the mountainous regions of northwest Africa a comparatively large but very lightly built horse evolved. Its tapering head with swelling muzzle and the unusual distance between the eyes and the nostrils give it a very striking appearance. These Barb horses characterized by their amazing stamina and sure-footed-ness have been cross-bred with Arabs, but basically they trace their descent from the desert mountains breed. The Islamic conquerors took the horses with them to south-west Europe. These horses were the basis for breeding the noble Andalusian horse which in the Baroque period was much prized throughout the whole of Europe. On the stud farms belonging to the nobility, the Andalusian was then used as the basis for developing such famous breeds as the Neapolitan, Lipizzaner, Frederiksborger, Knabstruppper and Klanruber. The American Mustangs are also descended from these Andalusians.

A small graceful finely-boned almost gazelle-like horse evolved on the bleak expanses of the deserts of south-west Asia. The grasses which thrived in their native habitat were not very lush so this type of horse did not need either particularly large or long teeth or very large digestive organs. There were no hiding places on the open terrain so a quick escape was always the best protection from hostile predators. They developed a fiery temperament which guaranteed a lightning reaction to danger. They also developed a broad thorax allowing plenty of room for efficient lungs and a strong heart. Their bodily structure and their natures were shaped by the climate, vegetation and condition of the terrain.

On the moors and glacial landscapes of the northern tundra a tough sturdy little horse eked out a bleak existence. This primitive pony had a broad rump, which allowed plenty of room for the robust digestive organs, long teeth specially designed to cope with being constantly worn down by grinding and a strong masticatory system which enabled it to feed on tough stringy plants, lichen and even the bark of trees. It is probable that this type of horse also had a coarse, fatty coat and a luxuriant mane and tail. The northern ponies are descended from this type. Most of the domestic breeds of pony retained their essential characteristics despite being cross-bred with other breeds; the Exmoor pony of south-western England has remained pure-blooded since the Ice Age.

A large massive horse with a heavy head also lived in the north alongside this small agile pony. It too could survive on large quantities of poor food. Some of these horses reached a height of about 17 hands. This horse is said to be the founding father of all the cold-blood types. These horses too were cross-bred with other types of horses; it is an indisputable fact that the breeding of warm-blood horses throughout the world would be unthinkable without the contribution of these cold-blood types.

Some types of ancient horse did not have to adapt to such extremes of living conditions. These horses were naturally domesticated much more frequently; Przewalski's horse, a steppe type, was the origin of numerous Asiatic breeds of horse. Mongolian horses, for example, have retained many of its qualities. In addition to other breeds of primitive horse, the tarpan, which was spread over Central and Eastern Europe, played a particularly important role in the development of the domestic horse. *(cited from: https://agecroft.wordpress.com/ancient-breeds-of-horse/)*

Natural Selection Transitions to Selective Breeding

Horses that were born with favorable traits, or adaptations, were more likely to survive, reproduce and pass on beneficial traits to their offspring. Over time, more and more horses in the population were born with adaptations that helped them to survive. This process of change over many generations is called natural selection. Charles Darwin was the first person to describe the process of natural selection. Based on fossil evidence, different types of horses evolved in different parts of the world.

The process of selective breeding occurs when humans breed horses to create offspring with a specific set of traits. Selective breeding is done only for human purposes but sometimes traits that people breed for are also selected for in nature.

The native habitat of both the small primitive pony and the massive ancestors of the cold-blood breeds was the glacial landscapes, moors and heaths of the northern tundra. [26]

The forest type was less specialized. It survived into the eighteenth century in the shape and had considerable influence on the breeding of the warm-blood horse. [26]

A very light long-legged horse with a striking ram-like head lived in the bleak mountainous regions of North Africa. It became the 'father' of the majestic horses of the Baroque. [26]

As the nomad herdsman evolved, so did the use of the animals they domesticated. It is probable that the horses they had herded for meat and milk were soon found to be more desirable as a pack animal than the reindeer, ox and onager they had previously domesticated and used as beasts of burden.

In the desert areas of south west Asia a type with fine limbs and built for speed evolved. It is called the primitive Arab. [26]

Eventually nomads of the steppes became agriculturalists and settled down. Their societies were matriarchal; young men were accepted into the tribes of their brides. A system of selective breeding possibly developed to improve meat, milk and wool production of their various livestock. With territorial expansions, skilled horsemen became warriors. One cannot be a warrior on an 11 hands high steppe pony; it is believed that around the 10th century BC breeding horses became a serious undertaking. The nomads moved around in hordes. As they moved around, better grazing became available for their herds of horses and so the horses improved and were essential to the skilled horseman turned warrior.

Although life in the steppe region did not demand any high degree of specialization, different breeds of steppe horse evolved. the grey small-headed, very lightly built steppe tarpan and the yellowish-brown heavier-headed Prjewalski's horse or Eastern steppe wild tarpan. [26]

Chin, in the Hsia district of China is often mentioned in ancient literature for it's wealth of horses. A "whip" (driver) by the name of Han Ngai is credited as the inventor of driving chariots in China. A similar type of chariot was introduced at about the same time in India, Iran, Mesopotamia, Syria, Egypt and Greece. Sources indicate that around 2000 BC the Hsia bred white horses with black manes for their chariots and their neighbors the Chou bred yellow (chestnut) horses with red manes. Sources also mention that the emperor's war chariots were drawn with white horses with black manes and were driven in pairs. This indicates that there was selective breeding occurring. Horse skeletons show that these horses were small with large heads and could have been related to Przewalski's horse. It is difficult to determine when there was a transition to riding from driving. Steppe tribes had already tamed the reindeer to ride but the steppe "pony" had to become big enough to ride.

All of this indicates that horse breeding was transitioning from natural selection to selective breeding. Throughout the known world at the time, societies were breeding horses that suited their needs; in other words, the form of the horse was being adapted to meet the needed function.

We are dealing with hundreds of thousands of years of evolution and it's only within the past five thousand years that we can type horses into the beginnings of breeds. In the wave of wars and invasions, cultures and horses mingled. The power of kingdoms was based on war chariots and later cavalries. The kingdom with the better chariots, cavalries and horses was the victor. It is probable that this was the greatest impetus for breeding form to function. *(cited from: https://www.texasgateway.org/resource/natural-selection-and-selective-breeding and "A History of Horse Breeding" by Daphne Machin Goodall and https://www.artbycrane.com/horse_breeds/light_horse_breeds/wild_horses.html)*

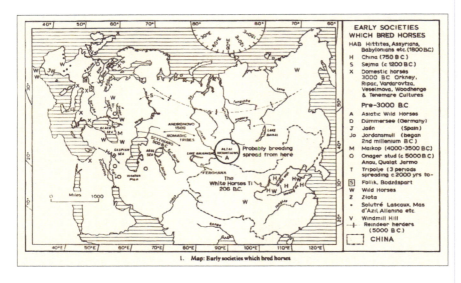

Early societies which bred horses [27]

The First Horse Breeders - Creating Form to Function

As with so many details of history, we'll probably never know when selective horse breding began. Breeding may have begun as far back as when horses were first domesticated. More likely though, when horses were first domesticated, they were probably used as they were found in nature.

As the needs of humans changed, cultures bred horses for a variety of purposes and a for a variety of qualities: speed (for messaging or racing), size and power (for war), heft (for plowing and wagon pulling), smoothness of stride (for riding), etc.

The 3rd millennium BC texts from some major sites in Syria (Ebla, Nagar, Nabada) indicate the importance of equids in the trade between the region's greatest kingdoms. There is not much direct evidence of horse breeding (as opposed to domestication) until the rise of the Bedouin culture of the Middle East. They began issuing written documentations of horse pedigrees around 1330 AD. Before that they possibly transmitted such information via oral tradition - for how long we don't know, but possibly for thousands of years. Farther east, Mongolian nomads had been breeding horses for centuries as well.

The elaborate panels at the southern end of the Apadana staircase in Persepolis are a record of nations, The panels show 23 delegations bringing their gifts to the Achaemenid king, Darius the Great (522-486 BC.) The Ethiopians begin the frieze in the bottom left corner and are joined by Arabs, Thracians, Kasmiris, Parthians and Cappadocians. The Elamites, Egyptians and Medians occupy the panel at top right. Note the size of horses. [28]

Warfare was a large factor in early selective breeding. The first evidence of equids in warfare dates from Eurasia between 4000 and 3000 BC. A Sumerian artifact from c 2600 -2400 BC depicts some type of equine in war and peace. By 1600 BC, improved harness and chariot designs made chariot warfare common throughout the Ancient Near East and the earliest written training manual for war horses was a guide for training chariot horses written about 1345 BC. As formal cavalry tactics replaced the chariot, so did new training methods, and by 360 BC, the Greek cavalry officer Xenophon had written an extensive treatise on horsemanship. The effectiveness of horses in battle was also revolutionized by improvements in technology, such as the invention of the saddle, the stirrup and the horse collar.

Many different types and sizes of horses were used in war, depending on the form of warfare. The type used varied with whether the horse was being ridden or driven, and whether they were being used for reconnaissance, cavalry charges, raiding, communication or supply.
(cited from: https://en.wikipedia.org/wiki/Horses_in_warfare)

The Horses of Antiquity
Misconceptions About Ancient Horses ~ Iberian, Barb and Arabian Horses

Sorraia horse [29]

The Barb (Berber horse) dates thousands of years before the Arabian horse and the Iberian horse several thousand years before the Barb. Noted equine historian Dr, Ruy d'Andrade has stated that the horse was domesticated in the Iberian peninsula as early as 25,000 BC. The horses portrayed in cave art in this area are very similar to the Sorraia horse. Daphne Machin Goodall in her book, *A History of Horse Breeding,* maintains that the early Iberian horse ancestor of today's Andalusian and Lusitano is a cross between the Tarpan and Przewalski. This cross resulted in Equus stenomius, a larger horse capable of carrying a rider unlike the Assyrian horses that had weak backs and were only suitable for chariot use. Equus stenomius is one of the six types of original wild horse known to man.

The last remaining herd of Equus stenomius still exits in the Portuguese Alentejo. It is the Sorraia. It exists in its original prehistoric state. The horse is small - 13 hands - but strong and with good temperament. The horse's methods of grazing and hilly terrain over which he traveled resulted in a thick arched neck and a strong, short coupled body. According to Goodall, the close connection of Morocco to the Iberian peninsula and the very similar conformation and coloring of the Sorraia to the Berber (Barb) make an interchange between the countries probable. In 400 AD Flavius Vegetius Renatus, in a veterinarian medicine book, states definitely that the African horse is of Spanish origin. From cave paintings it is clear that both convex and concave heads existed in ancient times. Claudius Aelianus (a Greek writer of the third century AD who wrote *On the Nature of Animals*) said of the Berber horses: "They are small and not very beautiful, but extraordinarily fast and strong and withal so tame that they can be ridden without a bit or reins and can be guided simply by a cane, so that only a lead rope is necessary on the halter." Much of the original Berber blood became mixed with Arabian after Islamic invasions of the seventh century AD but Berber characteristics prevailed: convex face, high wither, flat belly, sloping quarters with tail set low, very docile, quiet, strong with plenty of stamina. Symachus, a writer n the second century AD, said that Spanish horses were exported to Syria. Thus the Islamic invasions brought not only new Arab blood to the Iberian peninsula but also the old, related blood returned to Spain. Whatever changes were to take place during the Morrish conquest did not change the inherent genetic constitution of the Iberian horse. By the end of the Roman empire the Iberian horse breed was firmly established.

Arabian horse. Lithograph by Otto Eerelmand and Rich. Schoenbeck. Gloria Austin Collection.[30]

The Barb horse has often been confused with the Arab horse because old time writers incorrectly described inhabitants of North Africa as Arabs. Arabia lies in Asia and Barbary in North Africa; this is where the Moorish or Berber horses come from. The original Barb horse had no Arabian blood.

The Barb developed as a breed from the Sorraia which gradually migrated from Spain and Portugal to North Africa in pre-historic times over an ancient land bridge between the continents of Africa and Europe. Therefore, the Iberian horse is forefather to the Barb and not vie versa. According to Sylvia Loch in her book, *The Royal Horse of Europe*, at the time of the Morrish conquest, Barb blood was reintroduced to the Iberian peninsula.

The conformation of the Barb developed in the same way as the Sorraia due to the terrain of the area. The Barb was wiry, stocky, short-coupled and had incredible endurance. The Barb was fleet and hardy and built for handiness and agility. His short backed conformation enabled him to balance over difficult terrain. The Arab horse was also fleet and hardy and had sustained forward energy. The predominance of his weight was thrown onto the forehand, ideal for prolonged cantering without tiring over the endless plains of the desert. The Arabian horse did not exist until after the birth of Christ. By 700 AD, when Arabs invaded Numidia and Mauretania, it is likely that Berber horses received some Arab blood.

Numidia [31]

Nobody really knows about the early forerunner of the Arab horse. Archaeologists agree that horses did not exist in central Arabia before the Christian era began. Goodall believes that the likely source of the Arabian horse would be the decedents of the ancient Syrian and Assyrian chariot horses whose ancestors developed in the Steppes of Asia. In the time of Mohammed, the horse was a luxury: difficult to maintain and breed and not for use in battle. Camels were used for transport and for wars; it was by camel, not horseback that the Arabs first crossed frontiers to open the way of Muslim to the world. When Mecca fell, Mohammed's gains were 24,000 camels, 40,000 sheep but not a single horse. Of his invading army of 10,000, only 200 were mounted. Mohammed died in 632 AD. The defeat of the Berbers was in 702 AD and the entry of Moors and Arabs into the Iberian peninsula began in 710 AD. The first invasion into the Iberian peninsula was by Berbers with Barb horses. In 712 another invasion took place, this time there were more Arabs than Berbers. Moorish writers from the time indicate that the invaders said the Christian horses were bigger and better. The Moors captured the Christian horses for use in their cavalry. Spanish horses were so esteemed by the Moors that many were sent back as gifts to Arab rulers. For this reason, many historians feel that very little blood of Arabian horses was mixed into the Iberian horses. *(cited from: The Royal Horse of Europe by Sylvai Loch and A Hostory of Horse Breeding by Daphne Machin Goodall)*

Berber horse. Lithograph by Otto Eerelmand and Rich. Schoenbeck. Gloria Austin Collection. [32]

Iberian horse [33]

46

Horses of the Steppes

The Eurasian steppe stretches from Hungary in the west to Mongolia in the east and overlaps with four regions: Europe, Siberia, Central Asia and East Asia. Archaeologists have discovered

The Steppes [34]

new evidence of a horse-herding culture in the steppes of Central Asia where Kazakh ancestral tribes emerged more than 5,500 years ago. This is far earlier than the evidence for the domestication of horses or their use in war in Ancient China, Egypt or Mesopotamia. The steppe has linked Europe, the Middle East, Central Asia, China, and South Asia through economics, politics and culture since antiquity. Ancient steppe peoples embraced horsemanship with a skill above that of all other societies. Solid boundaries and enough space and grazing to support herds of horses that swelled into the thousands made this possible. In antiquity, people needed to remain close to freshwater sources in order to survive. Likewise, horses in the wild need water and grazing land; the steppe region provided this. The people of the steppes in ancient times were originally animists—believers that anything natural, like animals, the earth, stars, wind, water, and so on, had a spirit. When wild horses were first domesticated has not been determined. Estimates range anywhere from 4000 BC to 2500 BC. Archaeologists generally agree though it occurred on the Pontic steppe. Genetic studies suggest all modern domestic horses descend from the first steppe herds.

Originally nomadic, hunter-gatherers on the steppes hunted horses for food. As people gradually tamed the wild horse, they shifted into sedentary agricultural and pastoral communities, continuing to use the animal as a source of meat but additionally for hauling and plowing. Though no definitive date has been established, people gradually began to ride, allowing them to move more freely, much farther, and to manage herds more easily. Additionally, on the steppes pastoralists eventually realized that the harsh, endless grasslands were far better suited to grazing than farming. Building on their horsemanship skills and expanding their herds, equine-based cultures developed in which virtually the entire population was mounted. They spread from Hungary to Mongolia. A horse-culture is one in which the general population of a people was essentially all mounted - not just the elite.

Far to the east, in the first millennium BC, the Chinese warily watched pastoralists transform into mounted warriors who were expert bowmen. They knew this meant swift, repeated raids on the rich Chinese farmlands by mounted barbarian nomads. When bribery failed to keep the nomads at bay, the Chinese decided to adopt the same clothing, including trousers suitable for riding, learn horsemanship and become archers. Successfully repelling the nomads for a time, the Chinese then began to build defenses that they later incorporated into the Great Wall. The pastoralists expanded to the west too, along the Lower Danube valley, and on the Great Hungarian Plain within the Carpathian Basin. In places other than the steppes, horses were very expensive to keep. Poor grazing land prevented the existence of large herds of horses and also then prevented armies to have cavalries except in some areas of Thessaly, Thrace, Macedonia and parts of central Europe. An army would have had to cut hay and transport it as well as the supplementary grain. This was very time consuming. Beyond the steppes only the aristocracy, nobility, warriors and priests kept horses. These factors stalled chances of not only cavalry emerging but of the general population becoming a riding people.

It was not until about 1000 BC that powerful states emerged on the steppe itself. This became possible with the development of mounted combat, especially mounted archery. Mounted combat was innovated c.1000 BC, by peoples of the western steppe. Over the following centuries, it diffused to the eastern steppe and across Eurasia. The agility of mounted warriors made them far superior to chariots in the battlefield. The Mongol Empire (c.1200 AD-1300 AD) was the largest contiguous empire in history and represented the pinnacle of steppe power. The Mongol Empire encompassed the entire steppe and vast adjacent regions. At their peak, the Mongols controlled between eleven and twelve million contiguous square miles. In 1234 AD the Mongols, invaded China. By 1279 AD they were able to completely overthrow the Song Dynasty. Genghis Khan (1162 AD – 1227 AD), was the ruler of the Mongols at the time.

The key to their success was that they could move great distances in very short periods of time. Their horse archers seemed like they were coming out of nowhere. They were impossible to fight because they did not stay still long enough for any kind of engagement. The Mongol army's battle tactics depended on their sturdy, agile and durable horses. The Mongol armies respected their horses and took care of them. Every soldier had four to six horses. That way no one horse was ridden to exhaustion and that is why they could travel great distances; sometimes 60 to a 100 miles a day. Mongols were nomads so they spent their lives on horseback, herding and hunting. These skills were just what they needed for warfare. The Mongol army trained every day in horsemanship, archery, hand-to-hand combat and in battle formations and drills.

The agility of mounted warriors made them far superior to chariots in the battlefield. [35]

The fast, agile horses allowed them to have battle tactics that put them at a great advantage. One of these tactics was the pretend retreat. First, a small force of Mongols would charge the enemy. When the enemy would turn and retreat, they would be led right into an ambush. Another tactic the Mongols had was to pretend that they were retreating. The enemy would follow them and the Mongols would stay just ahead of the enemy until they found a battlefield they liked. Then the Mongols would turn and begin their next favorite battlefield tactic. With the enemy troops strung out over a distance, the Mongols turned to the attack. They encircled the enemy and rained arrows down on them then the heavy cavalry would move in for the kill. None of these favorite tactics would have been possible without the Mongol's horses. Since the Mongols were nomads, the horses were very important to their lifestyle. Anthropologists and archaeologists have found that the Mongol's horses were specifically bred for their lifestyle. Domestication was not a matter of training wild horses to obey commands. Rather, domestication involved genetic changes that

Mongolian horses today [36]

occurred over generations of selective breeding for particular traits such as obedience, size and comfort for the rider. The Mongolian horse is small like a pony, but it is not a pony breed. They have large heads, short necks, and wide bodies. They have strong, short legs with good joints and their hooves are sound and hard. Their stocky build makes them energetic, strong, and athletic. They have a high amount of stamina too. Horses that live in Mongolia today will spend time outdoors all year round. They are left to search for food on their own and they are used to surviving in temperatures ranging from -40°F to 86°F. While steppe tribes remained formidable enemies of neighboring civilizations for centuries, ultimately, the rise of the modern, gun-wielding army brought the age of the nomadic mounted warrior to an end.

The geographical features of the Eurasian steppe greatly contributed to the creation of European and Asiatic nomadic equine-based cultures in antiquity. Eventually most disappeared through conquest, assimilation into non-horse cultures or a return to sedentary ways. Due to its military campaigns against neighboring regions, the steppe had a monumental impact on Eurasian history. Some nomads continued to exist into later times, most notably the Huns and Genghis Khan's Mongolians in the medieval period. With the horse as a common link, elements of these ancient cultures were passed on in varying degrees to their neighbors. If the Eurasian steppe had not existed, horse-cultures might never have arisen at all. They could have developed elsewhere, but in different times and different ways. *(cited from: https://saberandscroll.weebly.com/uploads/1/1/7/9/11798495/5.2._a5.pdf and https://www.nationalgeographic.com/animals/mammals/facts/przewalskis-horse and https://www.edgekz.com/kazakh-steppe-land-horse-tamed/ and http://www.essential-humanities.net/world-history/steppe/ and https://erenow.net/ancient/the-horse-the-wheel-and-language/16.php and http://www.essential-humanities.net/world-history/steppe/ and http://www.china.org.cn/china/features/content_18389302.htm)*

The Equids of the Sumerians 2600 - 2400 BC

Sumer was first settled by humans from 4500 to 4000 B.C. It was located in the Mesopotamia region of the Fertile Crescent situated between the Tigris and Euphrates rivers.

By the fourth millennium BC Sumerians had established roughly a dozen city-states throughout ancient Mesopotamia, including Eridu, Nippur, Lagash, Kish, Ur and the very first true city, Uruk. Sumerians left behind scores of written records. They are renowned for their epic poetry, which influenced later works in Greece and Rome and sections of the Bible, most notably the story of the Great Flood, the Garden of Eden and the Tower of Babel.

Somewhere around 2600 B.C., a power struggle erupted between the leaders of Kish, Erech and Ur, which set off a "musical-chairs" scenario of rulers for the region for the next 400 years.

Ur was one of the first village settlements founded around 4000 BC and by 2800 BC it had become one of the most prosperous city-states in the region. The Standard of Ur is a box, the two large sides of which show aspects of life in early Mesopotamia. One side shows scenes of peace and the other scenes of war.

The 'war' side has three registers. The top register has one four-wheeled wagon pulled by equids, while the bottom register has another four vehicles with equids. The engravings offer some really interesting details about how these equids were observed and integrated into human activity. Starting with their tack, we can see that the animals were controlled by a nose ring. Reins were attached to the nose ring and run back to the driver through the rein ring. Actual examples of rein rings were found in the Ur tombs. Probably only one rein was attached to each nose ring. This method of control, combined with the kind of vehicle, would mean a rather unwieldy vehicle that would have been difficult to turn.

The equids on the standard have been called onagers, donkeys, wild donkeys and mules/hybrids. They do not appear to be horses. Beyond that, it is difficult from the iconography alone to establish with certainty what they are. There are such great variety in the sizes and shapes of equids that features like the length of the ears or the slenderness of the body can only be suggestive. Donkeys might be a good candidate since they are by far the most commonly attested equid at this period, but it is also around this time that a hybrid (the kunga) is first mentioned. It is not known exactly what it is a cross between, but the domestic donkey is almost certainly one of the parents. Whatever the case may be, these equids were highly valued and played a part (directly or indirectly) in human warfare from very early on.

The equids all have neck collars with some kind of tassels attached, probably a textile or leather. The tassels might mostly have been decorative, but could also have served a practical purpose; for example, keeping insects from bothering the animals, especially when sweating.

The rendering of the animals themselves is remarkable for its attention to detail and reveals good knowledge of their anatomy and behavior. The lines of the head and muzzle, main body, hooves and hocks are particularly accurate. Other features conform to the standard manner of rendering, as can for example be seen in the way the eyes are done on both humans and animals. Another interesting detail is the way the ears are shown, with one pointing forward and the other backwards. This is a very typical equine action that usually means the animal is paying attention to something, without being overly stressed or anxious. It is so characteristic that it must have been observed at some point.

Close up of Standard of Ur, War panel.[37]

There are equids being led along with a wagon. They wear a collar and possibly nose rings but otherwise no tack.

Sumerian chariot horse. Fragment of the Standard of Ur, War panel.[37]

Form to function is very interesting when looking at the equids on the Standard of Ur. The teams are shown at two different gaits. The 'peace' side equids and the two teams against the left edge on the 'war' side are all walking, while the remaining three teams in the bottom register appear to be charging or galloping.

The walking equids and other animals on the plaque are shown in a gait called the pace. This is a gait that some breeds of horses can perform. It is not natural to most equids and even less so at the slow speed of walking. Since all the walking animals

are shown in the same manner, it is difficult to determine if the equids were actually gaited or just depicted that way by a craftsman who may have not been knowledgeable about way of going.

The gallop or charging is equally problematic. An equid's canter/gallop has three beats, but the two front legs and the two hind do not move together as shown on the Standard. Might they instead be jumping over the fallen bodies underneath them? This would certainly explain the way the legs are depicted, but would the vehicles be able to roll over the bodies afterwards and keep upright?

Walking Equids. Fragment of the Standard of Ur, Peace panel. [38]

The accuracy of the rendering of the animals' way of going are in contrast with the anatomical details so does this mean that the way of going of horses at the time was as such or is this just artistically inaccurate? At any rate, The Standard of Ur presents us with some interesting perspectives into the form, function and type of equids used at the time.

(cited from: http://www.fao.org/livestock-systems/global-distributions/horses/en/ and https://www.history.com/topics/ancient-middle-east/sumer and http://teachinghistory100.org/objects/about_the_object/ur_standard and https://spiritedhorse.wordpress.com/2017/12/23/the-standard-of-ur/

Sumerian chariots. Fragment of the Standard of Ur, War panel. [37]

53

The Horses of the Ancient Greeks 1600 BC - 323 BC

The Minoans lived on the island of Crete in the Mediterranean Sea. Crete had been inhabited since 7000 B.C. The culture that developed there spread throughout the entire eastern Mediterranean world. Crete's command of the seas allowed its stunning art and architecture to deeply influence the Greek civilization that would succeed it. A volcano, followed by a tidal wave, devastated the island of Crete sometime between 1645 BC and 1500 BC. The once prosperous Minoans were now just a ragged people. Historians believe this one event changed the history of the ancient world. Eventually the island recovered and people from the city of Mycenae, in Greece, took over the island. The Mycenaeans were the first people from Greece to use horses in battle. With their weapons and chariots pulled by horses, they were able to take over the entire region of the Aegean Sea. They were the first great Greek civilization. Horses were of such great importance to the Mycenaeans that they were routinely sacrificed and buried in tombs with people since there was a belief that even without a rider a horse will always be a charger of the Gods but a man without a horse will only be a man.

Epitaph stelae (tomb inscription) depicting a horse. [39]

A recent discovery of a pair of yoke horses has been unearthed at Dendra, a prehistoric archaeological site situated outside the village with the same name belonging to the municipality of Midea in the Argolid, Greece. The site has a history stretching back at least to the early Bronze Age. If radiocarbon analysis of the horses' bone collagen verifies a hypothesis that they date earlier than the 16th century BC, historians will have to reconsider the established theory, that the domesticated equus entered Greece in the late second millennium. As ancient horses are unearthed, we learn more about their conformation and how they were used. We also learn what changes in conformation were achieved through selective breeding in order to perform desired functions.

Gravestone in Mycenae from 1500 BC - thought to be one of the oldest pictures of a chariot from that area. [40]

54

Two new, unplundered chamber tombs dating from the Late Mycenaean period (circa 1400-1200 BC), were unearthed at the Mycenaean cemetery of Aidonia in Nemea. The skeletal remains of a horse in grave 12 at Aidonia have been analyzed. The presence of two loose permanent incisors, their state of attrition, the lack of canine teeth and the shape of the pubic symphysis and obturator foramen allowed the estimation of the horse's age to three and a half to four years old, its sex as female and its height 130-135 cm. (12.3 - 13.1 hh). Hence the Aidonia horse in grave 12 was a young mare probably belonging to the so-called Elis breed, among the most ancient native breeds. Elis, also called Elea, modern Iliá, is an ancient Greek region and city-state in the northwestern corner of the Peloponnese, well known for its horse breeding and for the Olympic Games, which were allegedly founded there in 776 BC. The lack of macroscopic signs caused by the friction of metallic bits on the first premolar (verified with EM) suggests that the Aidonia horse had not been bridled prior to burial. Alternatively, it may have been a zygios or seiraphoros (yoke or trace horse) of a chariot, such as the synoris horses seen driven by two ladies on the fresco of the palace of Tiryns or at the mosaic at Hagia Triada. Yoke horses were not bridled often at that time. Instead they were controlled by head or neck collars devoid of bits. This fact coupled with the contemporary scene depicted at Tiryns (c.1300-1200 BC), the identification of the human as female, and the find of a signet ring in the nearby tomb 7 depicting a biga driven by unbridled horses allow the postulate that the sacrificial mare at Aidonia may have served as a

Skeleton of a sacrificed horse of Aidonia, tomb 41

Left: Two Ladies, Tiryns [42]

Right: Two Ladies, Hagia Triada [43]

Mycenaean Gold Signet Ring, Aidonia, 1500 BC.[45]

55

chariot horse during her short life prior to burial. *(cited from: https://www.archaeology.wiki/blog/2019/09/04/two-unplundered-tombs-discovered-at-aidonia-cemetery/)*

Horses of the ancient Greeks are often depicted with a slightly heavy but well formed head, thick strong neck, deep chest and strong hind quarters. Bodies are well filled out. Legs are slender and delicate and hooves are small. Manes and tails are luxuriant. Since the horses of ancient Greece were small (12 - 13 hh) it is probable that the first impression made by mounted riders must have been a vivid one, perhaps giving rise to the legend of centaurs. These creatures-half man, half horse-figure prominently in both Greek mythology and art. Theseus, the national hero of Athens, participated in a major battle between Greeks and centaurs that became a favorite theme for Athenian artists in both vase painting and sculpture. Theseus was also successful in repelling the Amazons, fierce warrior women who usually fought from horseback. They are thought to have come from the steppes north of the Black Sea, where it is now believed the horse was first domesticated, in the years around 4000 BC. Like the centaurs, the Amazons were a recurring and popular subject in Greek art.

Metope Centaur at Athens Acropolis Museum [44]

The rocky terrain of the Greek mainland was unsuited for wheeled vehicles and thus descriptions of the tactical role of chariots are rare. *The Iliad*, possibly referring to Mycenean practices of about 1250 BC, describes the use of chariots for transporting warriors to and from battle, rather than for actual fighting. Even after the abandonment of the chariot in the sixth and seventh century BC, the horse was used to bring the rider to the battlefield and then fighting was done on foot. There was a definite early prejudice against the idea of the use of the horse in warfare. This attitude changed considerably though after the Greeks became entangled with the Near East and were forced to view outside perspectives on warfare. To make full use of the horse's mobility, a lighter vehicle with spoked wheels had to be designed.

The rocky and mountainous geography of much of Greece was not well suited for horse breeding either. However, several regions in northern Greece were perfectly acceptable places for horses to be bred and easily kept, and so, the provinces of Boeotia, Macedon and Thessaly differed militarily from the rest of Greece. The best breeding of Greek horse stock took place in Thessaly, where prime existing stock was often crossed with Scythian, Persian (Nisean) and Ferghana horses. Thessaly is one of the few regions in Greece bestowed with broad and fertile plains. Regular summer rains and Greece's broadest stream, the Pineiós River and its tributaries, have made Thessaly's landscape ideal for the cultivation of surplus grain and the breeding of cows and horses on a grand scale. During the Mycenaean period, Thessaly was known as Aeolia. Thessaly made horsemanship their focus, rather then infantry and were known by their fellow Greeks as proficient horsemen worth fearing in battle. Because of their specialization in horsemanship, the best Hellenic horse breeds can be easily traced back to these three provinces. The horse-trade was highly prosperous for northern Greece and regional brands quickly developed to indicate particular horses of value. In Thessaly, for example, a breed developed called the Thessalian. This breed in particular was known for its high performance, endurance and large (comparative to other horses at the time) size. The breed's exceptional qualities were so famous throughout the whole of Greece, even in archaic times, that the Thessalian was mentioned in *The Iliad* as a superior horse. The legendary stallion of Alexander the Great, Bucephalus, was thought to be a Thessalian.

Bucephalus & Alexander
46

The ancient Thessalian horse was noted for its courage and beauty. A descendant of the Thessalian horse, known as the Pindos pony, is known for its hardiness. The old Thessalian breed developed by the Greeks had a rather coarse head; perhaps this is why Alexander's horse was called Bucephalus, ("ox head").

57

Their heads had a straight profile with wide eyes and small ears. They were small, strong horses. Their bodies were slim and their backs relatively straight, so the hindquarters were about level with the pronounced withers. Their legs had unusually short cannon bones. The Thessalians branded their horses. The overall conformation of the horse would suggest that the horse had a good climbing ability which would be advantageous in the rocky terrain of Greece. It is known that the animals from Larisa were branded with a centaur, those from Pherai with an ax, and those from Pharsalos with a bull's head.

Modern Pindos Pony [47]

The size of the horse may have been the reason that they were not used as cavalry but another reason was that the people were unfamiliar with cavalry tactics. Once introduced to cavalry, by invaders, the form of the horse changed, through selective breeding, in order to suit the new function as a cavalry horse.

Ancient coinage of Thessaly [48]

The small size of the horse can easily be seen, in relation to the riders, depicted on the frieze and pottery of the region. [49]

The dates of the Trojan war are debated; sometime between 1750 BC and 1184 BC. Homer wrote the *Iliad* and *Odyssey* sometime between 800 BC and 700 BC. Troy was famous for its horse breeding. Homer refers to Troy as a place where horses are bred and tamed. Hector was Troy's greatest warrior and Homer called him "tamer of horses". In his stories, Homer tells how much Hector loved horses. The Trojan War began when the Trojan prince, Paris, captured Queen Helen of Sparta. Helen's husband, Menelaus, convinced his brother Agamemnon, king of Mycenae, to lead an expedition to rescue her. Agamemnon was joined by the Greek heroes Achilles, Odysseus, Nestor and Ajax. They traveled in a fleet of more than a thousand ships. They crossed the Aegean Sea to Asia Minor to lay siege to Troy and demand Helen's return. The war lasted ten years until the Greeks decided to outwit Troy. Many Greek soldiers pretended to set sail for home, acting as if they had given up. In the midst of this pretend evacuation they made a large wooden horse and left it, as a supposed gift, at the gates of Troy. Troy loved horses so this seemed like an honorable gift. The Trojans pulled the mysterious gift into the city. When night fell, the horse opened up and a group of Greek warriors climbed out and opened the gates of the city to let the Greek army enter the city and conquer Troy.

The Trojan horse [50]

Greek horseman; Terracotta, 3rd century BC [51]

Another great author, Xenophon, was born in Athens in 430 BC. Xenophon was an author and also a military leader of the Greek mercenary army. He is well known for his writings about the world he lived in at the time. He wrote a lot about Athens, Sparta, Persians, generals and kings, as well as horses and dogs. All of his writings survive to the present day. Since most of his experiences involved battles it makes sense that two of his books would be about horses. *On Horsemanship* is all about owning and riding

59

horses and *On the Cavalry Commander* is about how to improve the Athenian cavalry corps.

Xenophon was the first person to teach people to respect a horse and to get to know the horse so that horse and human could communicate with each other in a good way. Many people today still use some of the methods taught by Xenophon. At the time that Xenophon wrote *On the Cavalry Commander,* war loomed between two Greek cities, Thebes and Athens. They had been at peace for some time so Athens was suffering from a decline in the quality of its cavalry. Xenophon hoped his advice on how to restore the cavalry to its previous excellence would help them become great again. Xenophon realized the effectiveness of the horse in war. He knew that the best war horse had to be bred, trained and treated very carefully. Until the time of Philip II of Macedon (reign 359 BC - 336 BC) mounted soldiers fought in a scattered, disorganized way, each doing whatever he and his horse were able to do according to his skill and his horse's skill. Philip demanded that his horsemen drill for their massed cavalry charges. Philip's ideas for how to successfully use horses was a big reason why he was able to conquer so many lands. Philip's son, Alexander, became an even greater soldier and leader than his father. At age 12, Alexander showed impressive courage when he tamed the wild horse Bucephalus, an enormous stallion

One of the most astounding discoveries in the 20th century was that of the late Prof. Andronikos, who found the un-looted Tomb II in the Great Tumulus of Aigai. He postulated that it may belong to Philip II, Alexander's father. There is an exquisite hunting scene on the fresco of the tomb's façade. Bones of four horses, two dogs, four bits, one pair of spurs and bridle parts, all charred, were also recovered from the tomb.

with a furious demeanor. The horse became his battle companion for most of Alexander's life. When Alexander was 13, Philip called on the great philosopher Aristotle to tutor his son. Aristotle sparked and fostered Alexander's interest in literature, science, medicine and philosophy. Alexander was just 16 when Philip went off to battle and left his son in charge of Macedonia. In 338 B.C., Alexander saw the opportunity to prove his military worth and led a cavalry against the Sacred Band of Thebes—a supposedly unbeatable, select army. When Philip was assassinated in 336 BC Alexander became the ruler until his death in 323 BC.

Philip is said to have imported twenty thousand Scythian mares to Macedon. His son, Alexander, claimed a tribute of fifty thousand Persian horses, which continued the infusion of Scythian, Nisean, Jaf, Ferghana and possibly Caspian and other blood into the Macedonian horses. Few of these horses were tall by modern standards, averaging 13.2 – 14.2 hands, with the possible exception of the Ferghana crosses and some of the Iberian stock. The Iberian horses mentioned by Homer were famed for their movement, size and spirit; the Nisean horses were known for speed and stamina, the Ferghana was noted for stamina, endurance and the ability to withstand hard conditions in desert lands. Along with imported stock, Philip had access to the native breeds such as the Pindos, Skyros, Pineias, Messara and Andravidas, horses known to be small but tough. Looking at the stock Philip used in breeding programs, one can easily imagine a hardy horse with stamina, endurance and longevity.

(cited from: https://ezinearticles.com/?Greece-Horses-in-Ancient-Greece&id=971992 and Homeric, British and Cyrenaic Chariots, J. K. Anderson, American Journal of Archaeology, Vol. 69, No. 4 (Oct., 1965), pp. 349-352 and https://trustedbyzantinemedievalcoins.wordpress.com/2021/04/04/horses-on-ancient-greek-roman-coins-including-races-chariots-pegasus-45/ and Horse Care as Depicted on Greek Vases before 400 B.C., Mary B. Moore, Metropolitan Museum Journal, Vol. 39 (2004), pp. 8, 35-67 and https://itchyfish.com/the-thessalian-rare-horse-breed-of-antiquity/ and coinage pictures By Johny SYSEL - Own work, CC BY-SA 3.0, https://commons.wikimedia.org/w/index.php?curid=28874395 and https://historandmor.blogspot.com/2016/08/the-thessalian-cavalry.html and file:///C:/Users/Mary%20Chris/Downloads/Horse_and_Horsemen_on_Classical_and_Hell.pdf and https://www.quora.com/What-breed-of-horse-was-Bucephalus?share=1)

The Horses of the Hyksos 1600 BC

The horse is not native to ancient Egypt and the exact date of its introduction to the country is not certain. There is considerable debate about when the horse was first used by the Egyptians. Some archaeological data which are presently available seem to undermine the claim that Egypt was without horses until the Hyksos arrived. For instance, a collection of 300 leather fragments of an Old Kingdom (c.2686 BC–2181 BC) chariot were rediscovered at the Egyptian Museum in Cairo. Another find in Nahal Tillah , a region of Israel's northern Negev desert seems to show that horses existed in the immediate vicinity. Many of the artifacts found have been Egyptian dating from 3300 BC - 3000 BC suggesting the Egyptians had horses earlier than 1600 BC. This fact made some scholars to opinate that it might be possible that the horse and military chariot were re-introduced to Egypt by the Hyksos. Most archaeological evidence found however attests that the domesticated horse was introduced into Egypt by the Hyksos from western Asia in the Second Intermediate Period (c.1650 BC – 1550 BC) at roughly the same time as the chariot.

The Hyksos settled in the Nile Delta from the Levant, looking for grazing land for their cattle. The Hyksos proved very difficult to expel from Egypt due to their competence with the horse and chariot, a method of warfare that the Egyptians had not seen before. But the horse soon became a much loved and prized possession for the Egyptian elite, particularly the Pharaoh. Ancient Egypt had her largest empire and greatest power due to the addition of the horse and chariot to Egyptian warfare. The horses first introduced to Egypt were smaller than those we are used to today. Yoke measurements from chariots found in tombs aid in speculating that the horses were 13.2 hands. However some horses probably measured up to 15 hands.

Tomb painting from Beni Hasan, Egypt. A figure named Abisha and identified by the title Hyksos leads brightly garbed Semitic clansmen into Egypt to conduct trade. Dating to about 1890 BC.

It is probable that a large stock of breeding horses were kept to make sure there was a constant supply for battle. Unlike donkeys, used for agricultural work from at least the beginning of the Pharaonic period (c.3100 BC), horses were essentially status symbols, used for such activities as hunting, warfare and ceremonial processions. They were almost always used to pull chariots rather than being ridden. However, battle scenes in the New Kingdom (1550 BC - 1069 BC) occasionally show individual soldiers mounted on them. *(cited from: https://www.touregypt.net/featurestories/chariots.htm and https://www.academia.edu/8814160/The_presence_of_horse_in_ancient_Egypt_and_the_problem_of_veracity_of_the_horseshoe_magic_in_the_ancient_Egyptian_folklore_and_mythology_pp_321_340)*

The Horses of the Mitanni and the Hittites 14th and 13th Centuries BC

The Egyptian era of peace and tranquility ended when the Hyksos invaded Egypt. The rise of Egyptian militarism coincided with the advent of the New Kingdom. Around 1650 BC, Queen Kamose defeated the Hyksos. The war against the Hyksos whetted the Egyptian appetite for battle. In the fifteenth century BC, Pharaoh Thutmose III had become Egypt's great empire builder, extending Egyptian control further and further east into Syria.

Early in the fourteenth century BC, Suppiluliumas I (1375 BC -1355 BC) created a new Hittite empire by defeating Kaska and Arxawa and eventually absorbed the Mitanni. As the Mitanni fought the Egyptians to the south, the Hittites advanced against the Mitanni from the north. The Mitanni threw back the initial Hittite advance, but increasing pressure from the north eventually pushed the Mitanni into an alliance with the Egyptians.

The two powers of Egypt and the Hittites were on a collision course and war finally erupted as the result of the political maneuvering of Ramses II. Despite the fact that the Egyptians had a much larger army, the Hittites had more chariots and better horses. The Battle of Kadesh in 1285 BC resulted in a draw between the two great super powers and in 1280 BC, the oldest recorded international agreement, was signed.

Battle of Kadesh [52]

The Hittites were very powerful and attacked many of the regions surrounding their sprawling kingdom. Their might continued to expand until they were a superpower on the level with Egypt and Assyria. They brought horses with them wherever they went and introduced the horse to many cultures. Their horses rank among the first horses in the Middle East.

The Hittite king, Suppiluliumas I turned the Hittites into an imperial force. The Hittites owed their military successes to their mastery of the war chariot. Techniques of bending and shaping wood helped the Hittites develop sophisticated two-wheeled models. The Egyptian horse drawn chariot typically consisted of a light wooden semicircular framework with an open back surmounting an axle and two wheels of four or six spokes. Two horses were yoked to the chassis by saddle-pads that were placed on the horses' backs. Leather girths around the horses' chests and bellies prevented them from slipping. A single shaft attached to the yoke pulled the chariots. Unlike Egyptian two-man chariots, the Hittite model could carry three people: the driver, a warrior armed with lances or bow and arrows, and a shield bearer. The latter was tethered to the back section of the carriage, lending stability during tight maneuvers.

Egyptian chariot [53]

Egyptian chariot at The Ketdkn of the north wall of the Hyposttlb Hall at Karnak, where Seti I. represents some episodes in his first campaign. And the Hittite king was absent in some other part of his empire. [53a]

Hittite chariot [54]

War chariot; Carchemish; second half of 8th c. BC; Late Hittite style under Assyro-Aramaean influence; Museum of Anatolian Civilizations, Ankara, Turkey. [54a]

64

The first known written information about horses was in 1345 BC; a Mitannian horse-master known as Kikkuli wrote the *"Chariot Training Manual".* It gave a detailed plan for training and caring for horses. The Kingdom of Mitanni spread from northern Mesopotamia down through Anatolia (which is modern-day Iraq through Turkey). The Kingdom of Mitanni had alliances with mighty Egypt. They both needed to protect themselves from the threat of Hittites. The Mitanni came from the East; they worshiped Indo-Aryan deities and their personal names had a similar origin. They brought with them their horses, probably the wiry, little horses of the desert and steppe. The Egyptians did not breed horses at the time but rather, horses were imported, captured in war or received as tribute. Through the eyes of artists, these horses appear to be small, elegant oriental horses - Equus orentalis (the Iranian mountain horse. This type conforms to the desert type. The breeds of horses of the Near East developed from this strain). *(cited from: https://www.nationalgeographic.co.uk/history-and-civilisation/2020/05/hittites-fast-war-chariots-threatened-mighty-egypt and https://www.historynet.com/battle-of-kadesh.htm)*

One of the most mysterious and powerful women in ancient Egypt was Nefertiti. Nefertiti was queen alongside Pharaoh Akhenaten from 1353 to 1336 BC. On the walls of tombs and temples built during Akhenaten's reign Nefertiti is shown alongside her husband more often than any other Egyptian queen. In many paintings she is shown in positions of power and authority driving a chariot. In this tomb painting in the tomb of Meryre, high priest of the Aten, Queen Nefertiti is shown smaller and follows the Pharaoh. Like him, she drives her chariot, drawn by a team of horses, whip in hand and without a driver. The famous horses of Nefertiti were probably Mittani.

The Horses of the Kushites and Assyrians c. 8th & 7th Centuries BC

The legendary Kingdom of Kush, with its series of capitals in what is now northern Sudan, helped define the political and cultural landscape of northeastern Africa for more than a thousand years. The Kingdom of Kush was probably the most famous civilization to emerge from Nubia. Three Kushite kingdoms dominated Nubia for more than three thousand years, with capitals in Kerma, Napata, and Meroë. As the New Kingdom ended and Egypt entered an Intermediate Period, power dynamics shifted in Nubia. Around 745 BC, the Kushite king Piye invaded Egypt, possibly at an Egyptian request to fend off invaders from Libya. Piye became the first pharaoh of Egypt's 25th Dynasty. Piye had a great respect for horses

By the late eighth century BC the Assyrians had developed a deep appreciation of horses. The Assyrians became an aggressive people under the rule of King Ashurnasirpal II who reigned from 884 to 859 BC. They were able to conquer many countries and kingdoms because they were the first to organize their army into units with commanders. They also built large powerful chariots that could be pulled by four horses. Cavalry and chariot forces were of utmost importance to their power. The Assyrians obtained their horses by booty and trade. Records indicate that they received gifts of large Egyptian yoke horses; the likes of which did not exist in their county. The Assyrians left many records about incorporating foreign chariotry and cavalry into their army.

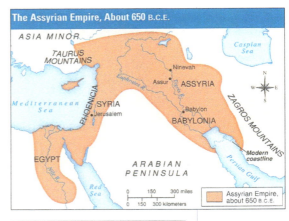

Assyrian Empire 650 BC [55]

Assyrian lion hunting relief from Nineveh, depicting grooms holding horses. [56]

Assyrian military campaign in southern Mesopotamia, horses and palm trees, 7th BC, from Nineveh [57]

These texts frequently mention Kushite horses. The Assyrians recognized cavalry as a new, powerful weapon of war. Innovations in the form of breeding horses, methods of harnessing horses and of importing foreign experts from Nubia and Samaria for chariotry, and Urartu for cavalry, contributed to their success. Nineveh was the capital of the Assyrian empire. The Nineveh Horse Reports were daily reports during the reign of Esarhaddon, king of Assyria 680–669 BC. The Reports detail the numbers and types of horses received in the capital by a governmental department from other cites and provinces in the Assyrian empire. The records indicate thousands of horses over a three month period. All of the chariot horses mentioned in the Nineveh Horse Reports are mentioned as being "horses of Kush" and the cavalry horses from Mesu (Iran). References to Egyptian and Kushite horses in Assyrian texts indicate that the two North African countries actively bred horses and that the horses of Kush were a breed prized by Assyrian charioteers.

Great armies need great and powerful horses.
The breeding of horses is now happening in earnest.

(cited from: https://www.nationalgeographic.org/media/kingdoms-kush/ and The Horses of Kush, Lisa A. Heidorn, Journal of Near Eastern Studies, Vol. 56, No. 2 (Apr., 1997), pp. 105-114 and Foreign Chariotry and Cavalry in the Armies of Tiglath-Pileser III and Sargon II, Stephanie Dalley, Iraq, Vol. 47 (1985), pp. 31-48

Assyrian horses bas-relief from Nineveh, 7th century BC.

Assyrian king Ashurbanipal on his horse thrusting a spear onto a lion's head. Alabaster bas-relief from Nineveh, dating back to 645-635 BC.

Marble slab from Ashurnasirpal II's palace. It is now in the British Museum. The image shows Ashurnasirpal II and his army advancing against a town. A battering ram is being drawn on a six-wheeled carriage.

During the reign of Assyrian king Tukulti-Ninurta II (891 BC - 884 BC) chariots were developed that had several new features. For the first time the chariot had a shaft of elliptical shape, which was designed to take stress from the pole to the car and also to control the balance of the chariot at full speed. These design changes may coincide with the introduction of a breed of horse that was larger and stronger than equids of earlier time. This horse was used for chariotry and cavalry in the reign of Ashurnasirpal II, (reign 883 BC - 859 BC) as demonstrated by the many depictions on the wall reliefs of that king's Northwest Palace at Nimrud. The animal's conformation is marked by a small head on a long neck, a sloping shoulder and a long slender body. The legs are long and thin and accentuate the height of the horse.

Assyrian chariot Detail on a wall relief from the Northwest Palace of Ashurnasirpal II

In the course of the eighth century, the Urartian kingdom became a powerful adversary of Assyria, effectively barring Assyria from importing horses from Urartian controlled territory. Thus later Assyrian kings had to obtain through tribute and conquest horses from the more southerly and distant regions in the western Zagros mountains, which included the land of the Medes. On a stele discovered in Iran, dated to 737 B.C., Tiglath-pileser III (744 BC - 727 BC) gives a list of Median chieftains with their respective tribute of horses, totaling over fifteen hundred equids. The Assyrian king, Sargon II (721 BC - 705 BC) imposed upon the Medes an annual tribute of horses.

Caspian horse pulling an Elamite cart. Detail on a wall relief from the Southwest Palace at Niniveh.

Many wall reliefs of horses paid as tribute to Assyrian king, Saragon II show them to be very small, under 10.3 hands. These horses appear to be Caspians, a small Middle Eastern horse whose conformation includes a refined, dished, small head with large eyes, long full mane and forelock, short back and fine leg. The Caspian was also known to the Elamites, as shown on a series of wall reliefs in a room of the Southwest Palace at Nineveh, dating to the period of Ashurbanipal.

Sennacherib was the king of the Assyrian Empire from the death of his father Sargon II in 705 BC to his own death in 681 BC. The utilization of larger Kushite chariot-horses during his reign was probably instrumental in the development of a bigger, large-wheeled chariot, which could now hold four persons. These horses were most probably home-bred under palace supervision. They are shown to be massive with sturdy conformation, each animal having a muscular body and broad neck, and of noble stature. All the animals exhibit a small-dished head notable for its alert expressiveness and rounded eyes.

Large Assyrian chariot horse. Detail on a wall relief from the North Palace at Niniveh.

After the collapse of the Assyrian empire, due in part to the hostile actions of the Medes, the finest and fittest horses bred in Assyrian-controlled territories in all probability spread to other parts of the Near East, to become the progenitors of later, equally fine breeds that include the Nisean and the Arab which is known to have originated in Western Asia.

(cited from: file:///C:/Users/Mary%20Chris/Downloads/Horses_of_Different_Breeds_Observations.pdf)

The stamina of the Kushite draft horses and their ability to move swiftly while pulling heavy loads are clearly demonstrated by the series of wall reliefs showing the episodic series of the royal hunt of lions in room C of Ashurbanipal's North Palace at Nineveh.

The Horses of the Medes and Persians 1000 BC - 88 BC

The oldest tribes of Iran are: Persae (Persians) and Madai (Medes), which appeared in the ninth century BC in the Assyrian inscriptions. Every spring, to begin their war season, the Assyrians either stole or demanded a tribute of horses from the Medes. Legend tells that King Medeus was the founder of the Median nation whose empire stretched across the East from Turkey, through Armenia and Persia to the lands of Afghanistan and Turkmenistan. The Medes were the greatest horse-breeders of ancient times; they bred their horses in the vast fertile plains of Nisa - in what is now Southern Turkmenistan. Horses were an enormous part of Median life. They even played a large part in their religion. Their chief god, Ahura Mazda, blessed men with good horses and good sons. Their sun god, Mithra, similar to the Greek god Helios, drove a chariot of four white stallions and he was referred to as being swift horsed and the lord of broad pastures. White Nisean horses were sacrificed to him at New Year and, like St. George, he was the protector of horsemen and chariot drivers. The great horses of Central Asia were legendary for their gaits as well as looks.

The Medes bred the Nisean horse, the finest horse the world has ever known. The breed is now extinct. The Nisean, was tall and swift and came in many colors; they were dark bay, white, chestnut and seal brown, but also were rarer colors such as black, roan, palomino and various spotted patterns. The Nisean was the mount of the nobility in ancient Persia. The ancient Greeks called the horse "Nisean" after the town Nisa where the horse was bred. Nisa was in Media which is now Turkmenistan. The Chinese called the horse the Tien' Ma "the Heavenly Horse".

Chinese Nisean spotted horse with estimated firing date between 900-1500 years ago of Tang, 618-906 AD [58]

"Man herding horses" by Han Gan 706-783 AD. Han painted many portraits and Buddhistic themed paintings during his career; however, he is most widely remembered for his paintings of horses. He was reputed to be able to not only portray the physical body of the horse, but also its spirit. His reputation rose and surpassed that of his teacher. Horse painters of later generations studied Han. He is honored with a crater named for him on Mercury.

The Nisean horse was the most valuable horse in the ancient world and they did not become extinct until the conquest of Constantinople in 1204 AD. Many Iberian type horses today are thought to be related to the Nisean.

Many breeds of horses were used by the Persians as their empire expanded. The governors of the many provinces in the empire provided hundreds of horses from their regions as tribute to their king. The Scythian horses, or ponies, were small and stocky with short manes. The Nisean horses were used for kings and generals to stand out on the battlefield and also demonstrate wealth and authority. The Persians thought that they could conquer Greece because the Greek city states did not get along with each other so all they had to do was prod them into war among themselves. Xenophon was one of the leaders of the Ten Thousand Greeks recruited by Cyrus the Younger, son of Cyrus the Great, to fight for Persia. Xenophon said that the Persians also had a finer horse known as the Armenian horse; now it is called the Caspian horse. It was very small; only about 12 hands. It was fast and agile with small ears and large nostrils.

Only chariot horses' manes were kept long. Horses that were ridden had short manes and tied tails to prevent interference from the enemy and weapons. Only the forelock was kept long and, in battle, was tied with a bright ribbon. Persian cavalry soldiers used large, bright, heavily embroidered saddle cloths. The cloth was secured to the horse with breast and girth straps that were knotted around spacers because buckles were still not invented. Stirrups were not invented yet either.

The Kara-Khanid ruler Ilig Khan on horse submitting to Mahmud of Ghazni riding an elephant, Persian painting, 1306-14 AD.
59

Alexander the Great advanced gradually and conquered Persia in 333 BC. Alexander's conquest of Persia is well documented. Needing replacement and refusing to ride just any horse,

Alexander went looking for the imperial stud farms, even holding towns hostage until they handed over the valuable horses. From Phrygia to Sogdiana, he captured horses and took them with him. Elwin Hartley Edwards, in his New Encyclopedia of the Horse, even called the famous Niseans of Ferghana, Alexander's Niseans.

After Alexander's death, his generals divided his empire among themselves. In 247 BC, a Parni Scythian named Arsaces overthrew the governor of Parthia. The main breeding grounds for the Nisean horse were under his control. Crowned king he quickly had to resist attempts to recapture lost territory. Being a son of Scythia, Arsaces was a superb horseman and he was about to revolutionize the way the great horses of Nisa were used. Instead of pulling chariots or acting as a simple cavalry, Arsaces developed the concept of heavy cavalry. Chain mail covered the great horses and riders, which required a new manner of tactics. Great horses became the ancient world's equivalent to tanks. Impregnable rings of metal protected man and horse.

The greatest Parthian king was Mithradates II who ruled from 123 BC to 88 BC. It was during his reign that Parthia came into contact with the Romans and the Chinese. Emperor Han Wu Ti's quest for Heavenly Horses is one of the most famous stories from ancient China. Acquiring them from a fort at Kokand in modern Uzbekistan put the Chinese into contact with the Sogdians, allies of Parthia and ancient history's most important middlemen. This opened up the Silk Road, a caravan route that carried silks and other goods to the West; horses and alfalfa among other items to the East. An interesting fact is that alfalfa, an important feed for the Nisean horse, was introduced to Greece at this time; it should be noted that wherever the Nisean horse was taken, alfalfa followed.

Heavenly Horse. Ceremonial bronze finial with standing horse, 4th-1st century BC. This artifact from the Greco-Bactrian Kingdom. As the Scythians came into contact with the Greeks in the Greco-Bactrian kingdom, artists from the two cultures influenced each other. [60]

(cited from: http://dictionary.sensagent.com/Nisean%20horse/en-en/ Nisean and https://www.horseoftheamericas.com/TheyHuntedTigers.htm and https://www.shorthistory.org/ancient-civilizations/mesopotamia/persian-empire/the-term-persia-and-medes-empire/)

Horses in China 2nd Century BC

Ancient China did not have enough good quality horses because the climate was not good and there was not enough fodder. Their neighbors, the people of the Steppe region, had wonderful horses. The Steppe region of northern central Eurasia was known in ancient times for its horse breeding and horse-riding nomad peoples. The nomads of the Steppe regions had many well-bred horses. These nomadic barbarians were excellent horsemen and archers. On their agile horses they could move in swiftly and make attacks on China. The Chinese were indeed more cultured but they were at a disadvantage when it came to protecting themselves. The horse had such an important influence that some historians think that the Great Wall was built against the horse, since the country lived under the constant threat of invasion from the nomads of the Steppe region with their swift horses.

Dayuan, or Tayuan, was a kingdom in Central Asia in the Ferghana Valley from 250 BC to 125 BC. The Dayuan were the descendants of the Greek colonists that were settled by Alexander the Great in 329 BC. The land of Dayuam had been ruled by Greek generals and overlords for hundreds of years, after the death of Alexander the Great, as part of the Seleucid Empire. Dayuan possessed the most amazing horses known to the Chinese at the time. The Ferghana horse was also known as the "Heavenly Horse" in China or the Nisean horse in the West. During the continual wars among growing empires in Asia, achieving power depended on the ability to fight on horseback. The art of cavalry required the strongest horses. Emperor Wu Di (reign 141 BC - 87 BC) wanted to trade bolts of silk for a thousand horses and march them back to the Han court. However, it was easier said than done. The horses were considered national treasures so the Dayuan refused to trade or even sell the horses. In 138 B.C., General Zhang Qian, the commander of the guards at the imperial palace, volunteered to make the dangerous journey to Central Asia to make peace with nomadic tribes in order to trade silk for their horses.

Dayuan or Tayuan [61]

General Zhang set off with a hundred mounted men. They were ambushed and captured and remained in captivity for ten years. When General Zhang Qian saw the horses they had, he was stunned by their beauty and strength. They stood 16 hands and were superior in muscle and stamina to China's horses. The general finally managed to escape and return to the Han court. He described the magnificent steeds to the Emperor. So began the first war ever fought over horses. It was called the War of the Heavenly Horses. Wu Di sent out Li Guangli with 6,000 horsemen and 20,000 infantry soldiers. Li's army had to cross the Taklamakan Desert and his supplies soon ran out. After a gruesome march of over 1,000 miles, he finally arrived to the country of Dayuan, but what remained of his army was exhausted and starving. After a severe defeat at a place called Yucheng, Li concluded that he was not strong enough to take the enemy capital and therefore returned home in 102 BC. Emperor Wu Di then gave Li Guangli a much larger army along with a huge number of oxen, donkeys and camels to carry supplies. With this force he had no difficulty reaching Dayuan this time. After a 40 day siege, the Chinese had broken through the outer wall and cut off the water supply. The people of Dayuan eventually offered the Chinese all the horses they wanted. Li accepted the offer and went back home with 3,000 horses.

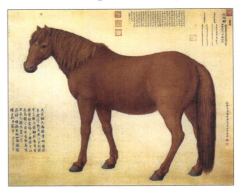

Ferghana horse by Giuseppe Castiglione, a Jessuit painter in the Chinese court - 1748 titled A Horse named Dawanliu.[62]

A rubbing of an image of Ferghana horses (or "heavenly horses") discovered in a tomb dating back to the Han Dynasty period. [63]

Ferghana horses were one of China's earliest major imports. The interaction between the Dayuan and the Chinese is historically crucial, since it represents one of the first major contacts between an urbanized Western civilization and the Chinese civilization, opening the way to the formation of the Silk Road that was to link the East and the West in material and cultural exchange from the 1st century BC to the 15th century. *(cited from: https://dailyhellas.com/2019/10/21/ancient-greco-chinese-war-of-the-heavenly-horses/)*

Sweating Blood Horse Coin cast during the Song Dynasty.[64]

Celtic Horses

The Celts spanned across a wide geographic area and included numerous cultures and ethnicities. Because of this fact, the traditions, practices and lifestyles of Celtic speaking peoples varied considerably. Trading between Celtic tribes was well established before Romans came to Britain.

The first horses of the region probably arrived there on their own by walking there with or without the assistance of Stone Age man. From cave paintings it can be seen that some horses in the region were small measuring at 11 hands much like Shetland ponies and some were fine boned similar to the horses used by the Hittites. There were also large boned 14 to 15 hand horses with convex heads. Many were a Tarpan offshoot that developed into the Exmoor pony. They are believed to be the direct descendants of the horses that walked onto Britain before it was an island. Archaeological evidence dating back over 60,000 years bears an uncanny similarity to the Exmoor Pony of today. Fossil remains trace the existence of horses on Exmoor to 50,000 BC. The ancestors of the modern Exmoor Pony existed in relative isolation on the moor, maintaining the breed's genetic integrity. Even today, these ponies still possess a close morphological resemblance to the primitive horse. The Exmoor Pony is small but hardy, with a height of only 11.1 to 12.3 Hands. The breed's short legs, stocky build, and strong jaw suit the rugged terrain and coarse vegetation of its habitat. Their dark bay or brown coats consist of a dense undercoat to insulate them from freezing winter temperatures. There is also a long, oily, outer layer to protect them from chilling ice and snow. The fleshiness of their eyelids gives further protection from the cold. Additionally, the docks of their tails include long,

Exmoor ponies [65]

Horse from the Lascaux caves made by the Cro-Magnon peoples at their hunting route in the Stone age. [66]

75

coarse hairs known as a "snow chute". These are designed to deflect water away from their groin and belly. "Mealy" markings of buff coloring around their eyes, muzzle, flanks, and belly also characterize the Exmoor Pony. These coat traits are also known as primitive "Pangaré" markings. They are found in other horses, such as the wild Przewalski's horses of Mongolia.

Around 500 BC a powerful tribe know as the Brigantes began to import horses from northwest Spain for the purpose of chariot driving. Warfare and the traditions surrounding war were one common thread of similarities throughout Celtic societies and cultures. The importance of horse ownership and warrior status was shared by the Halstatt Culture which developed in the region and lasted from around the 12th century BC to the 6th century BC when it was succeeded by the La Tene Culture. Burials tell us a lot about the development of warrior culture. Warrior burials are distinguished from more ordinary burials in prehistoric cemeteries by the richness and significance of their burial rites. Important individuals were distinguished by the inclusion of items like horses, horse tack and weapons. Vehicles such as carts and chariots were also included in high-status burials.

Tribes and cities in Gaul at the time of Julius Caesar.[67]

The Celts were renowned for their skill on horseback and horses played an important role in Celtic culture. The importance of horse ownership and charioteering to social status and wealth in Celtic culture is a testament to the role of mounted warfare in Celtic Europe. Roman sources describe the Celts bringing both wagons and chariots into battle. According to Romans, the Celts used their chariots to get into the fray and intimidate their

Reconstruction of a Celtic chariot.[68]

enemies before jumping off and fighting on foot. Each mounted warrior would be accompanied by two grooms who each had a horse in case their master's horse was wounded. If the warrior was wounded, one of the grooms would return him to their camp, while the other one remained to fight in his place. (*cited from: https://www.magnaceltae.com/post/ancient-celtic-warfare and https://ihearthorses.com/exmoor-pony/*)

In late July 390 BC, Rome was sacked by Celtic invaders from Gaul who burnt and sacked the city. The Romans considered the Celts to be barbarians. Their long hair and mustaches were strange looking to the Romans. They were fearsome fighters. This was the first time that the Romans encountered the Celtic cavalry. The horsemen of the Celtic cavalry had most likely been riding since childhood. Thousands of fearless and yelling horsemen invaded a stunned Rome. On the Capitol Hill a small number of Romans put up a valiant defense, holding out until famine forced them to surrender.

Eventually Rome became powerful again but most people who lived in Italy were afraid of invasions from Gaul. Gaul is the name given by the Romans to the territories where the Celtic Gauls lived. The people who lived there were made up of a multitude of states of different ethnic origin. Gaul included present France, Belgium, Luxemburg and parts of the Netherlands, Switzerland, Germany on the west bank of the Rhine, and the Po Valley in present Italy. The horses of Gaul were small compared to those of Italy. Horse-breeding was an important part of Celtic culture. Horses were used both for riding and as pack-animals. Trade and commerce increased throughout Gaul thanks to the use of the horses. The different cultures of the many states of Gaul started to mingle and become one culture. Eventually people from Germany started to migrate into Gaul. The Germans were fearless in battle. In battle, a swift German light infantry soldier ran alongside each cavalryman, clinging to the horse's mane to keep pace. He protected the cavalryman's flanks and stabbed at the enemy horse.

The Roman Republic stood strong for several centuries. However, as Rome's power and territory expanded, internal wars began to arise as citizens and families fought among themselves for power.

During these civil wars, Julius Caesar began gaining much power. He commanded the loyalty of the soldiers in his army. Julius Caesar decided to end the threat from Gaul and conquer the territory. In his conquest of Gaul, Julius Caesar relied on the magnificent horses and riders of Gaul and Germany. It was not unusual for those who felt looming defeat to join the army of the conqueror. Caesar valued these warriors. Time and time again they lead Caesar to victory on their small but mighty horses. Caesar said that a pair of the Celtic horses yoked to a chariot was so active and well trained that the horses could be turned in a narrow space or pulled up when going at full speed on a steep grade or even made to stand while the warrior ran out on the pole and stood on the yoke. From what Caesar described, the horses were under 12 hands. The Celtic ponies were also often gaited - a valuable asset for mounted horsemen without stirrups. These ponies were favored for their gaits and breeding of those that could do the four beat lateral gait was promoted. Today descendants of these smooth riding ponies still exist in Iberia (Garrano pony) and Iceland (Icelandic horse).

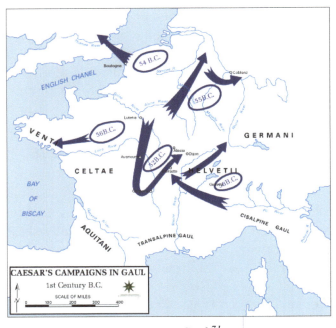

Maps of Caesar's campaigns in Gaul. [71]

Garrano pony [69]

Icelandic horse [70]

Roman Horses

Rome was a small city state in the 6th century BC and was governed by kings. After only seven kings had ruled the city the people who lived there managed to overthrow the kings and create a republican government that would represent the wishes of the Roman citizens. A senate was put in place to rule over Rome. By around 300 BC, real political power in Rome was centered in the Senate which at the time included only members of patrician and wealthy plebeian families. Once Rome became a republic, it grew in strength and went on to conquer much of the Mediterranean. Rome's military conquests led to its cultural growth as a society. The Roman Republic lasted from 509 BC to 27 BC. The second period was the Roman Empire which lasted from 27 BC to 476 AD. During this time the government was led by an emperor. The Roman Republic collapsed as a result of internal problems, unlike the Roman Empire which collapsed as a result of external threats.

After the Celts sacked Rome, the Romans improved their military and became very powerful. Road systems often sprang up after Roman conquest of a region. The Romans built new highways to link captured cities with Rome and establish them as colonies. The Roman road system was made up of about 50,000 miles stretching from Syria in the east to Britain in the west. Caesar once covered 800 miles in ten days on one of the Roman roads. A person on horseback could cover 360 miles in two and a half days. Horse and mule carts averaged five to six miles per hour. This speed of transportation remained unequaled until the 19th century. Roman roads were very easy to travel; they had road signs and mile markers. They also had state-run hotels and way stations. The most common of these ancient rest stops were the horse changing stations which were located every 10 miles along most routes. These simple post houses consisted of stables where government travelers could trade their winded horse or donkey for a fresh mount.

Since Rome was a military empire, the horse was an essential element in communications, transportation and fighting. The empire was vast and wherever the army went, the horses needed to be fed and watered too. The solution was aqueducts. Aqueducts are a complex network of ground works, pipes and other structures designed to transfer water from a source to a destination. Rome's aqueducts supported a population of over a million. Once built, aqueducts had to be maintained and protected. The excellent planning of the ancient Romans made sure that maintenance requirements were part of the plans. Repair people could get to underground sections of the aqueducts by means of manholes and shafts. They even had a way to divert water away from a damaged section until it was repaired. Some of the aqueducts are still in use today.

Mons (Var) Aqueduct from Mons to Fréjus partly rebuilt, home to the so-called modern springs. [73]

The reconstructed Roman Eifel aqueduct near Mechernich, Germany. [72]

Until recently, excavations had not found any stables in Roman forts. In 1998-2000 excavations found that soldiers and hoses actually lived together in the same building. There was a natural bond between these mounted warriors and their horses. The soldier and his mount rode together and lived together in a tight-knit community, realizing that, as Xenophon advised, "It is plain that in danger the master entrusts his life to his horse."

At the peak of the Roman Empire it included most of mainland Europe, Britain, much of western Asia, northern Africa and the Mediterranean islands.

Excavation of a Roman fort. The stone walls outline where the barracks would have been. Horses lived in the grassy area in the middle. The long pit collected horse urine and would have been covered with boards or stone slabs to keep the floor dry. [72a]

80

Outside the major cities of the Roman Empire people lived a simple life on farms, dependent almost entirely on their own labor. The horses were not only used to pull plows in the field but also as sacrifices to the gods for a plentiful harvest. After a race to decide which horse was to be sacrificed, the blood was used to purify livestock, the tail was brought to the king for health, and

Map - The Roman Empire 1st Century B.C. to A.D. 150. [74]

the head of the horse was nailed to the wall in hopes of a bountiful harvest. The countryside played an important role in the economy of the Roman Empire. Many different foods were grown in different areas and then shipped throughout the empire on the vast network of Roman roads.

Rome made a great sum of money from their trade within their empire. Roads were useful in transporting troops as well as facilitating trade.

Roman road in Pompei. [75]

81

Life in the cites was much different. For the affluent, the day was divided between business and leisure. Business was only conducted in the morning. Most Romans worked a six-hour day, beginning at dawn and ending at noon and some shops reopened in the early evening. The afternoon was devoted to leisure - attending the games the theater or the baths - all of which were also enjoyed by the poor because many in government felt the need for the poor to be entertained. Even during times of crises, the citizens of Rome were kept happy with games. Chariot racing was one of the most popular spectacles. The Circus Maximus was a chariot racetrack in Rome. It was originally built in the 6th century BC. It also hosted the Roman Games (Ludi Romani) which honored the god Jupiter. These were held every September with fifteen days of chariot races and military processions. The Circus Maximus had room for 250,000 spectators.

Circus Maximus [76]

The Circus Maximus had:
- a track covered in sand about the length of five football fields
- twelve starting gates for chariots at the open end of the track.
- a decorated barrier called a spina complete with obelisks running down the center of the track.
- tapering turning posts placed at each end of the track.
- lap markers in the shape of eggs and dolphins which were turned to mark the completion of each of the seven circuits of a typical race.

Charioteers were like our movie stars today. They were very popular and became very rich. Horses became famous too. Just like the Kentucky Derby today, horses for the chariot races were specially bred. Race horses were bred and trained on private and, later, imperial farms. When ancient Roman records mentioned horse breeds the Numidian breed was mentioned most frequently. Other breeds used were the Spanish horses. The training of a race horse would begin about the age of five and their careers could last up to twenty years. After their racing careers, if they were successful, they were used for breeding.

The chariots were pulled by teams of four, six, eight or twelve horses. The lead horse in a chariot race was often as famous or more famous than the driver. Fans knew the breeding line and all the details of their favorite horses. Teams of four horses were called a quadriga, meaning four yoked. The two outside horses were called the funalis and the two middle ones were the iguales, or the actual yoke horses. The funalis were the faster horses who would set the pace, while the iguales were the ones who pulled the weight of chariot and kept it steady. All the horses would need to work as a team and match pace with each other and take signals from their driver on when to slow down and when to speed up.

A bad horse would have spelled disaster for the whole team. The inside funalis horse was the one closest to the spina; he had the most difficult job because he had to lead the team around the sharp turns while keeping the fast pace. When a specific horse was named in a quadriga in ancient records, it would usually be the inside funalis horse. Some of the names of hero race horses were: Abigieus, Lucidus, Cotynus, Galata, Pompeianus. The names mean nothing to us now, of course, but the mere mention in the stadium of "Abigieus" would drive the people crazy. Horses needed to be very strong and fast and agile too! They needed enough speed to gallop the straightaways and still be able to negotiate the dangerous turns at the turning posts; that is where most chariots would overturn. The chariot, driver and horses had to complete seven full laps around the Circus Maximus for a total of about five miles.

In later years of the Roman Empire, the Roman emperor Caligula owned a retired, unbeaten chariot horse named Incitatus. Incitatus had a stable made of marble and a stall made of ivory. He wore only purple blankets, the color of

Incitatus [77]

royalty, and had jewels hanging from around his neck. The horse had its own servants and its oats were mixed with gold flakes. The emperor would issue invitations, on the horse's behalf, inviting dignitaries to dinners attended by the horse's servants and would host lavish birthday parties in the horse's honor.

Ancient Rome was a kind of society where class structure not only existed but was strictly enforced. The distinction between the upper and lower classes was clear in the ancient Roman class structure. Patricians were the upper class people who wielded political and administrative power and enjoyed wealth. Lower classes, known as plebeians, indulged in all sorts of work but did not have the political and administrative power of the upper classes. However, it was possible for members of the plebeian class to become the political elite. For instance, Roman Emperor Augustus was of plebeian origin. Apart from the distinction between the patricians and plebeians, there was a very important distinction between the senatorial class and the equestrian class in ancient Rome. The senatorial class consisted of all the men who served in the senate and wielded political power. The equestrian class, on the other hand, was of economic importance and any man who could prove that he possessed a certain amount of wealth could be enrolled in the equestrian order. It was also possible for a member of the equestrian class to become a senator, in which case he became a member of the senatorial class. A member of the equestrian order, known as an Eques, was required to serve up to ten years of service in the cavalry between the ages of seventeen and forty six.

The Praetorian Guard was one of the most distinctive features of Roman imperial rule. Only the best, most deserving and physically-trained soldiers were accepted into the guard. Half were foot soldiers and half were cavalry. They were equipped with the latest weapons and they underwent extremely difficult training in ancient martial arts. Augustus formed the Praetorian Guard. He recruited fifteen cohorts of about five hundred men each. Each cohort eventually swelled to one thousand men. Three of the nine units were stationed in Rome while the other six were stationed throughout Italy. Each cohort was under the command of an Eques. The elite cavalry arm of the Praetorian Guard formed the personal cavalry bodyguard of the Roman Emperor but they also functioned as a police force both in Rome and other Italian cities. The Praetorian Guard was responsible for the overthrow or murder of fifteen out of the first forty-eight emperors who governed Rome between 27 BC and 305 AD. Constantine saw the danger of trusting the Praetorians any further and disbanded the units that remained, scattering the soldiers all over the empire.

Descriptions of what constituted a good cavalry horse do not vary much between the Republic and the late Empire. While farmers and merchants made do with local horses that were adapted to their needs and circumstances, the Eques were in agreement on where the best horses were raised and on the qualities of a good warhorse. The Roman army valued the horses bred by the Celtic tribes which formed the core of the auxiliary cavalry units. Breeds favored for cavalry mounts also included those from Libya and Spain. Ancient historians Vegetius, Livy, and Strabo all agree - cavalry horses should be fast, calm, rugged and obedient. Most Roman cavalry horses were around fourteen hands. The size and power of a horse were secondary considerations. The average horse would be on the small side compared to modern horses, but this was not considered a handicap in war; ancient cavalry tactics were built on maneuvering and raiding more than charging.

Statues could help to tell us about the "look" of ancient Roman horses. There were many statues of horses in ancient Rome. Ancient sources tell us that there were twenty-two "equi magni"—colossal bronze equestrian statues—that decorated the imperial capital. The statue of Marcus Aurelius is the only one left standing today. The other twenty-one equi magni were melted down during times of war or strife. This single statue was preserved because it was incorrectly identified as the later emperor Constantine, who reigned from 306 AD to 337 AD. To later Christians, Constantine was an important historic

Marcus Aurelius [78]

figure so the statue was not melted down. *(cited from: http://www.legendsandchronicles.com/ancient-civilizations/ancient-rome/ancient-roman-class-structure/ and https://hadrianswallcountry.co.uk/learning/ideas-and-inspiration/hadrians-cavalry/cavalry-horses and https://www.reddit.com/r/AskHistorians/comments/2mrsps/were_horses_smaller_in_ancient_times_namely/)*

Review of Horse Types of Antiquity
To sum up, there existed the following types/strains of horses:

Equus Przewalski - the Asiatic wild horse/ Mongolian horse [79]

Equus gmelini - the Tarpan [80]

Equus europiums or Equus celticus, the plateau horse/ Exmoor pony [81]

Equus robustus - Delle/ Cob [82]

Equus orientalis - Arabian type, Caspian pony [83]

Equus stenonius, the horse of Spain and North Africa/ Berber, Sorraia [84]

86

The Horses of the Middle Ages
Monks and their Mounts

The horse defined the Middle Ages! Horses, along with mules and donkeys, were relied on for transportation, agriculture, war and recreation. A large part of the population was dedicated to occupations that used or cared for horses. In the Middle Ages roads were no more than dirt tracks that often turned into mud. Some goods were carried by pack horses and carts. Men traveled on horseback and ladies traveled in wagons covered in painted cloth. The wagons looked pretty, but they were very uncomfortable on bumpy roads since wagons of the Middle Ages had no springs. Travel in the Middle Ages was very slow; they could only travel thirty to forty miles a day.

In the Middle Ages the Christian church was growing due to the missionary work of monks. Trade routes were also very busy during the Middle Ages; the world became very interconnected. Many who sought to dedicate their lives to the Church went to study, live and work in the monasteries. Over time monks, who normally stayed in their monasteries praying, became missionaries too. Monasteries became centers of learning. Priests often traveled between churches and monasteries preaching. Monasteries also welcomed travelers; it was an opportunity for the monks to teach their visitors about Christianity. Monasteries often had stables for the horses of their guests. Many monasteries also kept their own horses so that they could travel and preach as needed. Horses were bred by Carthusian Monks beginning in the late Middle Ages. Some of the earliest written pedigrees in recorded European history were kept by the Carthusian monks. Since they could read and write, they kept careful records. They used the finest Spanish Jennets as a foundation for the horses they were breeding. The horses bred by the monks were highly sought after by many people, including kings! Through the years the Carthusian monks guarded their bloodlines with passion, even denying an order to breed horses owned by royal stud farms into their stock. El Cid's famous horse Babieca was bred by the Carthusian monks.

About eighty two percent of the Pura Raza Espanola (PRE) horses in Spain today contain some Carthusian blood. [85]

Horses of the Knights

Until the Norman conquest in 1066, the people in England lived on their own farms. They owned the land they lived on. William declared that he conquered the land and it ALL belonged to him. He divided the land up and gave it to the knights who had helped him conquer the land. These knights became known as lords. The lords gave some of their land to other knights who would fight for them. They also gave land to peasants and serfs who had to give part of everything that they raised on the land to their lord. Everyone in England served someone else; this system is called feudalism.

"Right handed" knight [86]

During the Middle Ages horses were classified by their use, not by breed like we do today. The most valuable horse in the medieval stable was the horse of the knight, the **Destrier.** The word destrier, meaning "right-handed" comes from the fact that the knight held a lance under his right armpit, passing it over the horse's neck on its left side in order to hit his opponent. The horse needed very special training. The horse needed to run directly towards another rider. That is a very unnatural thing for a horse. The horse also had to learn to gallop on the right lead. That means that the right front leg advances and touches the ground to a greater extent than the left one. This was necessary so that the horse could be ready for an impact coming from its left. The momentum of the moving horse actually gave the blow its power so it was important that the horse was fast as well as strong so that he could accept the blows as well as help his rider deliver the blows. The Destrier was a very valuable horse so the knights even had rules to protect their horses. In tournaments, there were penalties if a horse was purposely hurt by an opponent. There is a general misconception that these horses must have been massive but they weren't.

Armor for man and horse by Kunz Lochner, Nuremberg, 1548. Horse armor belonged to Johann Ernst, Duke of Saxony [87]

88

If you go to a museum and see some actual armor from the Middle Ages, you will be surprised that the horses were no bigger than most riding horses today; the destriers were about fifteen to occasionally sixteen hands. That may seem small but that is still larger than most of the other horses of the Middle Ages. Most horses in the Middle Ages were the size of large ponies.

Other Horses of the Middle Ages

Knights only used the destrier for battle and tournaments. Most knights also had other horses. **Coursers** were light, fast horses. They were the most common medieval warhorses. They were more expensive and better quality than Rounceys, but not as expensive as Destriers. Coursers were sometimes preferred over Destriers in battle. The Courser was better for hard battle and fast pursuit because of their speed and stamina. Coursers were also used for hunting. Hunting was reserved for the noble class. Often times animals were hunted with dogs that were scent or sight hounds, depending on the animal they were hunting. The most popular hunted animals were deer, boar, wolves and hares. Hawking was also a popular form of hunting. Hawking or Falconry was the sport of hunting small wild game or birds with trained birds of prey like hawks, falcons and eagles. Coursers were used as messenger horses too. Messengers were a vital link to court and government communication. They accompanied envoys to court, and they apprehended criminals so they would need a good fast horse.

Mounted on a destrier, Richard Marshal unseats an opponent during a skirmish.[88]

Hawking or Falconry, The Devonshire Hunting Tapestries, late 1420s. [89]

The **Rouncey** was the most affordable horse and usually the animal of choice for a poorer knight or squire. Rounceys were rather plain, general purpose

89

horses who were also used for riding and as pack horses but never for pulling carts. They could also be trained for war. Rich knights supplied their attendants with Rounceys. They varied greatly in characteristics; virtually any sound and reasonably fast horse was called a Rouncey.

The ideal riding horse was the **Palfrey.** Palfreys could equal a Destrier in price, and for good reason; they had an extra gait known as the amble, which was fast, comfortable, and could be maintained by both rider and horse over long distances. This made traveling much easier and more pleasant. They were usually small horses, probably no taller than fifteen hands. The horse of choice for noble ladies, the Palfrey was probably quite pretty. It was used almost exclusively by nobility because of its high price tag. Palfreys are also sometimes called Jennets.

Rouncey [90]

Chaucer's Wife of Bath rode a Palfrey [91]

Food and goods in the Middle Ages were all transported by either pack horses or cart horses. The pack horse was faster than the cart horse, so it was used to transport perishable goods. The **Sumpter** was a grade horse used as a pack horse. Knights even used Sumpters to carry their armor when it was not being used. Most people think these horses were very small – pony size. There aren't that many illustrations of Sumpters but in England today there are plenty of native ponies that were used extensively for hauling on the pack routes.

The **Hobelar** was a rugged and hardy pony which later became known as a "hobby" horse; they were also used as cart horses. The highest demand for cart horses was the transportation of hay and timber. Unlike pack horses, cart horses were used to move bulky or oddly shaped items. Cart horses were very important for moving goods around the cities. Most carts were light, two wheeled vehicles.

In the beginning of the medieval era, the horse played only a small part in heavy farming duties. Oxen were preferred due to a lack of appropriate harnessing systems for horses. The Chinese invented the full collar harness in 100 BC but that invention did not make it to Europe until 700 AD. The full collar was one of the most important inventions in human history. It allowed the horse to maximize its pulling power by better load distribution so that now the faster horse could be used for farming instead of the slow oxen.

Peasant Farmers [92]

At first, horses and oxen were commonly intermixed. Innovations such as horseshoes, whiffletrees, tandem harnessing, traces and better vehicle design helped to increase wider spread use of all horse teams. The ox was stronger, cheaper to maintain and less temperamental but it lacked speed and endurance. The horse could work fifty percent faster and up to two hours longer a day since they didn't need to rest to digest food. The horse used for farming was called an **Affrus** or **Stott.** They were usually smaller and cheaper than the cart or pack horse.

Affrus or Stott used in a 13th century farming scene, 1279. [93]

By using the faster horse in combination with an improved plow and better farming practices, peasants could produce a surplus. Having a surplus enabled peasants to trade at markets on weekends. Markets then evolved into towns. Towns allowed

91

people to give up farming and allowed a living by buying and selling surplus goods. There was a belief that, "the city air makes you free." Eventually more people did not need to live by subsistence farming. This led to the growth of cities and allowed the development of early industry, education and the arts.

While life on the farm was improving, transportation by wheeled vehicle was not. Most people in the Middles Ages either walked, rode or used a litter. There was little need for road networks in a rural, feudal and self sufficient society. The roads that did exist were not maintained; they were overgrown, dry and dusty in the summer and quagmires in the winter.

14th - 15th century work during July. [94]

Farewell of Johann Frederick I of Saxony of Emperor Charles V, 16th century. [94a]

Lady in Horse-litter, returning from Tournament. 15th century. [95]

Wheeled transport was uncomfortable and more strenuous than riding horseback since the body of the vehicle sat directly on the axle. Consequently, transportation by wheeled vehicle was at a very slow pace. Furthermore, in the medieval mindset, it was an insult to manhood to ride in a carriage. Only women, the infirmed or the dead rode in carriages. A journey by carriage was dangerous since the slow moving vehicle was subject to robbers and the horses risked broken legs on the bad roads. Nobles traveled a lot during the Middle Ages. When they traveled, they took everything with them from one place to another. Sometimes they would need as many as four hundred horses to move themselves and everything they needed for a long trip!

Detail of a miniature of Ermengarda in a carriage, with the castle and Pont de Fin of Lille, the giant Finard slaying Salvard, and Ermengarda received by the hermit. [96]

Nobles traveling to Nonsuch Palace as seen in a hand-coloured engraving from Braun and Hogenberg's Civitates Orbis Terrarum, 1582. [97]

93

The Horses of the Age of Discovery 1350-1780

Things around the world were starting to change. Rather than loot and destroy, conquering armies were trying to mingle and learn new things from the people that they conquered. People were beginning to assimilate into the culture and there was an exchange of ideas. A new era of cultural, artistic, political and economic rebirth was about to begin. The Renaissance (1350-1650) and the Age of Enlightenment (1650-1780) were part of the Age of Discovery.

At the end of the Middle Ages, cites began to develop as subsistence farming was no longer necessary for the masses. With the rise of a middle class, there was an emergence of specialized horse breeding for specific purposes just as the Mongols had been doing. Beginning in the Renaissance, horses were bred for sporting endeavors as well as for war. Horses would be ridden for pleasure and used for transportation by carriage; horses were bred specifically for those purposes too. Improved farming methods called for a larger and stronger horse to be developed which led to the development of draft breeds. The world was coming out of the Dark Ages into a Renaissance and horses were going to continue to play an important role. The horse was even going to be an important part of the New World.

St. Geroge and the dragon, dated 1348. [99]

So many of the paintings and drawings until the Renaissance don't look real and they are out of proportion.

During the Renaissance sciences advanced and that included including the knowledge of anatomy. Painting techniques and products improved too. Oil paints and tiny brushes were developed and layering techniques were developed that gave paintings depth. Not only did artists portray horses in a more realistic way but people also began to think of the horse in a more realistic way; horses were a part of every day life so horses needed to be bred

St George and the dragon dated 1504. [98]

that could accomplish various tasks in the most efficient way. Wars, agriculture, travel and even pleasure all contributed to the evolution of horse breeding. Purpose-bred horses for specific traits, such as speed, endurance and strength were developed.

Horses of the Ottoman Empire

Since the Mongols were nomads, the horses were very important to their lifestyle. Anthropologists and archaeologists have found that the Mongol's horses were specifically bred for their lifestyle. Domestication was not a matter of training wild horses to obey commands. Rather, domestication involved genetic changes that occurred over generations of selective breeding for particular traits such as obedience, size or comfort for the rider. On the eastern side of the Byzantine Empire was the Seljuk Empire. This Empire had been invaded by the Mongol leader Genghis Khan. The Mongols divided the area into states with many different leaders. One of their leaders was a man named Osman. Osman was a Seljuk Turk. He was a magnificent horseman and fencer. The name "Ottoman" comes from his name.

Ottoman mail and plate armor for horse and soldier, 16th century armor as worn by fully armored cavalryman (sipahi) [100]

The Ottoman Army was the most feared army in Europe. The real strength of the army, and the fiercest warriors, were the horsemen known as the Sipahis. The Sipahis were professional mounted warriors granted land from the Sultan. The Sipahis did not breed horses for money. They were bred because it was a state requirement. The rivalry between the Sipahis for the best horse provided for an increased quality of horses. The horses were bred for speed, strength, calmness and intelligence. The superior discipline, organization and size of these armies, compared to their European opponents, made them almost unbeatable for three centuries of warfare. The Ottoman Empire was one of the largest empires in history. It was in existence for six hundred years; the Ottoman Empire continued to exist until the first World War in 1914.

Horses of the Cossacks

In 1462 Ivan the Great became the Grand Duke of Russia. Ivan the Terrible was the grandson of Ivan the Great and was the Tsar from 1533 - 1584. Part of Ivan's army was made up of a group of people called "Kasaks" (Cossacks). The Cossacks were horsemen from the Russian Steppes who were descendants of the Mongol Golden Horde. They were free roaming outlaws who robbed and raided the countryside. In 1552 Ivan asked the Cossacks to join his army to defeat the Tartars. The Tartars were the combined forces of Mongols and Turks. The Cossacks joined the Russians and helped give the Russians their first victory over the Tartars in one hundred seventy years. Cossacks became an important part of Ivan's army and remained important throughout Russian history. At this point in history, people became interested in breeding horses in order to create horse breeds with specific abilities.

Russian Cossacks on horseback, circa 1900.
101

From their many raids the Cossacks began to gather horses from all parts of the area. The horses that were able to survive the lack of food and water in the harsh elements and endure the rigors of battle were used for breeding. It was indeed "survival of the fittest" that was important in their breeding program. The horse they produced was a medium-sized, rangy, agile and brave horse of astounding endurance and vitality. The horse became known as the Don horse.

The Beginning of Horse Breeding in England

The Hundred Years War was actually longer than one hundred years; it lasted from 1337 to 1453. There were periods of peace and plague in between the many battles of the Hundred Years War. It all started over claims to the throne that pitted the kings and kingdoms of France and England against each other. One hundred years is a long time so during that time there were improvements in battle strategies and technology. Then, just when the English had finished the Hundred Years War, they started to fight among themselves. The War of the Roses was a civil war for the throne of England. It was the War of the Roses that inspired William Shakespeare's play "Richard III". Richard III battles Henry Tudor for the crown at the Battle of Bosworth. In the play, Richard's horse is killed in the middle of the battle. He then wanders to find it in the battlefield for hours, yelling. "A horse, a horse! My kingdom for a horse!" The war lasted from 1455 to 1485 and in the end a new royal dynasty emerged - the Tudors.

In Tudor times the royal household was divided into three departments. These departments were 1) the household above stairs, otherwise known as the "Chamber", 2) the household below stairs which included the kitchens and domestic responsibilities and 3) the stables. The men responsible for these three departments were the Lord Chamberlain, the Lord Steward and the Master of the Horse. These three men were considered to be the "Great Officers" of the King's court.

The Master of the Horse was appointed by the King. He was responsible for the King's horses and stables. It was his job to provide the King with horses for war, racing, hunting and litters. They did not drive coaches then because the roads were too rough so when the king did not ride a horse, he was carried in a litter. The Master of the Horse was also responsible for all the people that worked or held positions in the stables. He was responsible or the King's hunting dogs as well as the King's falcons too. Since the king spent a lot of time with his horses, the Master of the Horse held a position on the Privy Council. The Privy Council was made up of the King's closest advisors.

By the time of the Tudors, warfare in England was starting to change. New weapons of war, early cannon, war ships and heavy-duty castles and forts meant the use of horses in open battle was decreasing. Horses started being used more for sport and status. Henry VIII was the first English King to race horses.

England lost many horses during the War of the Roses so, Henry VIII passed several laws in relation to horse breeding and started to import thousands of horses from abroad; horses were imported from Italy, Spain and North Africa. Henry had royal stables for breeding horses for hunting and racing. He set up stables at Greenwich where his horses were trained and their stamina and speed improved. Until now horses were only of a "type". Now horses were starting to be bred for specific qualities and traits. Henry VIII was interested in improving both type and size of British horses. Laws passed in 1535 and 1541 required that all mares should reach thirteen hands high and stallions fourteen hands. Nobles kept certain numbers of horses. Those in the highest positions had to house seven strong trotting horses who were at least three years old and fourteen hands high. The less wealthy had to have at least one acceptable horse. In 1540, horses less than fifteen hands high were forbidden from grazing on common grounds and removed to enclosed land where they would not breed with larger horses. In addition to the demand for bigger, stronger horses, it was important to make sure that there would always be enough quality horses available for war.

King Henry VIII followed by Sir Anthony Brown, Master of the Horse. From the Cowdray Engravings portraying the King's visit to Portsmouth, July 19, 1545.
102

The Thirty Years War and the Emergence of the Finnhorse

Gustavus Adolphus was the king of Sweden from 1611 to 1632. He is credited with founding the Swedish Empire and led Sweden to military power during the Thirty Years War. The Thirty Years War (1618-1648) began as a religious civil war between the Protestants and Roman Catholics. The war soon developed into a struggle for the balance of power in Europe. When the Catholic forces seemed likely to win, first the Danes, then the Swedes and finally the French intervened against the Hapsburgs. In 1630, Sweden, under the leadership of Gustavus Adolphus, took the side of the northern Protestants and joined the fight. By the end of the war all Germany was ruined and half its people were killed. For more than two hundred years, Germany remained divided among local rulers and at the end of the war, France emerged as the dominant power in Europe. By the end of the Thirty Years War it became obvious that there would not be one religion for all people. People wanted to be able to choose what faith they wanted to follow – they wanted individual expression. This is what started the Age of Enlightenment.

Swedish intervention in the war was a major turning point of the war. During the war Gustavus Adolphus showed his kingdom's military capability. He had new tactics that amazed the world. He adapted his army to the new technologies of cannons and guns and he began to rely on fast moving light cavalry units to attack the enemy lines. His soldiers also became fabled. Among is warriors were cavalrymen from Finland. They were brave and brutal and had a war cry: "Hakkaa paalle" which meant "hack them down". They became known as the Hakkapeliittas. The Hakkapeliittas looked funny in the eyes of the soldiers from other countries. They wore breastplates and helmets. They were armed with carbines and two pistols and they had sabers for close quarter combat. The Finnish horses of the Hakkapeliitas were small compared to other horses on the battlefield so the Hakkapeliitas were not taken seriously because of the small horses. Soon, they were proven wrong. The horses were fast and highly maneuverable. The horses used by the Hakkapeliitta were the ancestors of the modern Finnhorse.

Gustavus Adolphus and the Hakkapeliitas [103]

99

France and the Breeding and Training of Horses

Cardinal Richelieu (1585 -1642) made France the greatest power in Europe. He was able to use the Thirty Years War to further the national interests of France. Richelieu became the Chief Minister of King Louis XIII in 1624. Louis XIV became King of France when he was only four and a half. He was king from 1638 to1715. Louis XIV is best known for the magnificent palace that he built at Versailles. He loved horses and built extravagant stables at Versailles. The Versailles stables could house over seven hundred horses and had over thirty carriage buildings. At the end of his reign he had one thousand seven hundred horses.

In the Small Stables at Versailles, the horses were organized according to whether they were used by the King or for carriages. In the Great Stables there were hunters which were ridden for hunting and there were riding school horses. New ways of horse riding were introduced in the stables at Versailles. The new methods showed kindness to the horses. Almost all of the horses in the stables at Versailles came from England, Ireland, Spain, North Africa and northern Europe. The horses were considered to be the most elite collection of horses any place in the world at the time. In political terms, a King's horsemanship skills were a symbol of his ability to govern well.

Louis XIV crossing the Pont Neuf in Paris in a carriage in front of the statue of his grandfather Henry IV. [104]

In France the Master of the Horse was called the Grand Écuyer. In addition to all of the duties of the Master of the Horse in England, this person in France was also in charge of horse breeding and training young nobles to ride. One of the most famous Grand Écuyers was Antoine De Pluvinel (1552 -1620). He wrote a book entitled, "L'Instruction du Roy en l'exercice de monter à cheval". It was about teaching the king how to ride. Many people still read his book today. He is best known for his kind training methods. Much of dressage today is based on his ideas and methods.

Just like in England, there was now a national pride in breeding horses specific to the needs of the country and often, the wishes of the nobility. One of the most famous French breeds that was perfected during this time period was the Percheron. Many believe they are the product of multiple breeds that came to France: Arabs during the Moorish invasions, the great Flemish horses of the knights and the Boulonnais horses (thought to have been a horse from the time of the Romans). Breeding these many horses in the Perche province of France resulted in the Percheron. Back then they were much smaller than the Percherons of today. They were between fifteen and sixteen hands and more agile. They were almost always gray. Paintings and drawings from the time usually show French nobles and other important people on great gray horses.

A mid-19th century painting by Rosa Bonheur, depicting a French horse fair that includes Percherons 105

101

The Influence of Spanish Horses

In Spain, the monarchs, Ferdinand II and Isabella I, created an enormous empire by uniting several independent provinces. Ferdinand was king from 1479 to 1516 and Isabella, his wife, was queen until her death in 1504. The Spanish empire spread east from Spain to include the kingdoms of Germany, Hungary, Bohemia, Naples and Sicily. It also extended south and west to include possessions in North Africa and the Americas.

In 1501, Louis XII, the King of France at the time, declared that he had the right to be the ruler of Naples, Italy. He went into Naples and split the kingdom with Ferdinand. The deal soon fell through and they went to war over the kingdom. In 1504 Ferdinand was victorious. While Ferdinand was in Italy the Italians saw the magnificent Spanish horses for the first time. The Spanish horse had a natural ability for quick turns, lightning fast departs and a willing and friendly nature. The horse could perform amazing "airs above the ground" during battle. The horse trainers of Naples could not get their less talented, heavier horses to perform the same beautiful "airs" as the Spanish horses. From the beginning, the Spanish horse was bred and used as a war horse. He had to be able to turn on his haunches quickly to face an opponent or to sprint away from the danger to protect his rider. In those days the horse was the reason for life or death. The horses were built for speed and agility. Since the warrior would spend days on end on the horse, the horse had to be comfortable to sit on and have a soft stride.

The entire European nobility rode Spanish horses during the Baroque age. [106]

On September 28, 1527 King Philip II of Spain published a decree that a new horse breed should be created. He wanted to breed a distinctly magnificent horse. Philip II founded the State breeding real Yezuada de Castilla (Royal Horse herd). Spain was at the height of its power. The conquistadors conquered South and Central America and the Spanish horse became the world's most popular riding horse; the demand from abroad was so outrageous, that it created difficulties to satisfy the requests. The Spanish horse left its footprint in the entire world. At the beginning of the 16th century, the Spanish governors of Cuba and Venezuela took their noble Spanish horses to their new areas of domination. In 1502 the first Spanish Governor of Santo Domingo brought his ten Andalusian horses on the island. At the same time, the entire European nobility rode Spanish horses during the Baroque age.

In 1532 Frederic Grisons' first riding academy with Spanish horses emerged in Spanish Naples and in 1594, under Pluvinel, the School of Versailles opened. In 1565, the Spanish riding school of Vienna was formed on the present Joseph square within a wooden riding area, which later was replaced by a magnificent building. Since at this time there were only Spanish horses ridden, the Institute got the name "Spanish riding school". These beautiful horses are still bred in Spain today and are known as Pura Raza Española (PRE) horses.

Austria - The Hapsburgs and Horses

During the Renaissance, Vienna, Austria, was a leader in science and fine arts. Austria was ruled by the House of Hapsburg from 1273 to 1918. The House of Hapsburg, was one of the most influential and distinguished royal houses of Europe. During the Renaissance Charles V, of the House of Hapsburg, was the most powerful monarch in Europe. He inherited Spain, which had been united by his grandparents Ferdinand and Isabella. He succeeded his paternal grandfather Maximilian I as Holy Roman Emperor. He was Duke of Burgundy and Archduke of Austria and he also ruled the Netherlands, Bohemia, Hungary, Naples, Sicily and Sardinia. Ruling Spain meant ruling Spanish America and in Charles's time Cortés conquered Mexico and Pizarro conquered Peru.

A supposed famous quote of Charles V is: "I speak Spanish to God, Italian to women, French to men, and German to my horse." By this he meant that: Spanish was considered the language of religion, Italian as the language of love, French as the language of diplomacy and of many Royal courts and German as the language of the empire, of which the horse represented strength and conquest. He obviously knew how important the horse was to his empire.

Charles' health began to fail so he abdicated. He handed the running of the Holy Roman Empire over to his brother Ferdinand in 1554 and in 1555 he resigned the rule of the Netherlands to his son Philip of Spain. The following January he resigned Spain and Spanish America to Philip. In August he formally abdicated as Holy Roman Emperor. Charles hoped that Philip would eventually rule his whole empire, but the empire was too big to manage. Ferdinand and his son Maximilian refused to accept Philip's succession and the Hapsburg dynasty split into Austrian and Spanish branches.

One of Ferdinand's sons was Charles II, Archduke of Austria. In those days marriages were arranged in order to unite kingdoms. Arrangements were made for him to marry Elizabeth I of England and when that fell through, arrangements were made to marry Mary Queen of Scots but that fell though too. In 1571 he married his niece. They had fifteen children. It was a good thing he did not go to England or Scotland because his influence on horse breeding in Austria was very important.

The Hapsburg family controlled both Spain and Austria when the art of classical riding became important in Europe during the Renaissance. There was a need for light, fast horses for use in the military and for the classical riding that was being taught to nobles. In 1562, Maximilan brought the Spanish horse to Austria and founded the court stud at Kladrub. His brother Archduke Charles established a similar private imperial stud farm with Spanish horses at Lippiza. The Kladrub and Lipizza horses were bred to the local Karst horses and then crossed with Neapolitan horses and other Spanish horses from

Stud farm in Kladruby nad Labem - Kladruber horses [107]

Spain, Germany, and Denmark. The Kladrub stud produced heavy carriage horses. Riding horses and light carriage horses came from the Lipizza stud.

The Spanish Riding School in Vienna is still in existence today breeding and training Lippizan horses. It is named after the early Spanish horses imported by Charles II. It is the oldest surviving riding and breeding facility of its kind in the world. Its purpose has remained the same since then - to preserve the art of classical horsemanship.

Spanish Riding School, 1890. Winter Riding School arena, Vienna, Austria. [107a]

Spanish Riding School, 2003. Winter Riding School arena, Vienna, Austria. [108]

When the Ottoman Empire took control of Constantinople in 1453 they blocked European access to the area and also blocked access to North Africa and the Red Sea. This severely limited trade. Europeans needed to find new trade routes.

Up until this time most sailors kept well within sight of land or traveled known routes between ports. Prince Henry the Navigator (1394 -1460) changed that. In 1419, Prince Henry started the first school of navigation at Sagres, Portugal. The goal of the school was to train people in navigation, map-making and science to prepare them to sail around the west coast of Africa. He encouraged explorers to sail beyond the mapped routes and discover new trade routes.

Portuguese explorers discovered the Madeira Islands in 1419 and the Azores in 1427. Over the coming decades, they would push farther south along the African coast, reaching the coast of present-day Senegal by the 1440s and the Cape of Good Hope by 1490. Less than a decade later, in 1498, Vasco da Gama would follow this route all the way to India.

In 1519 Magellan set sail in his attempt to find another route to Eastern Asia. He led the first expedition to sail all the way around the world. He also discovered a passage from the Atlantic Ocean to the Pacific Ocean that is today called the Straits of Magellan.

While the Portuguese were opening new sea routes along Africa, the Spanish also dreamed of finding new trade routes to the Far East.

Prince Henry's School of Navigation, Artist: Mielatz, Charles Frederick William (Breddin, Germany, 1860 - New York, 1919) [109]

Complete citations and references are at back of the book. Some citations for the sections on Horses of the Middle Ages and Age of Discovery are listed here but are not limited to these sources:

https://cartujano-pre.de/en/cartujano/die-pferdezucht-philipps-ii/ https://www.encyclopedia.com/history/encyclopedias-almanacs-transcripts-and-maps/rise-monarchies-france-england-and-spain

https://www.history.com/topics/inventions/printing-press

https://worldhistory.us/european-history/the-rise-of-nationalism-during-the-renaissance.php

https://www.historylearningsite.co.uk/france-in-the-sixteenth-century/louis-xi/

http://american_almanac.tripod.com/louisxi.htm

http://www.sdopera.com/Content/Operapaedia/Operas/Rigoletto/FrancisIofFrance.htm

https://en.wikipedia.org/wiki/Grand_Squire_of_France

http://countrystudies.us/spain/7.htm

https://www.bartleby.com/essay/The-Accomplishments-of-Queen-Isabella-and-King-PK7SSJ6SWGDSX

https://web.archive.org/web/20141217041847/http://www.ialha.org/our-breed-2/how-andalusians-friesians-lipizzaners-and-lusitanos-are-called-baroque-horses/

http://theborgias.wikifoundry.com/page/POWERFUL+FAMILIES+of+Renaissance+Italy

https://www.ducksters.com/history/renaissance/italian_city-states.php

https://myarmoury.com/feature_armies_italy.html

https://en.wikipedia.org/wiki/Neapolitan_horse

https://www.britannica.com/biography/Charles-V-Holy-Roman-emperor

https://www.chronofhorse.com/article/history-spanish-riding-school-vienna

https://www.britannica.com/place/Vienna/History

https://www.history.com/topics/reformation/martin-luther-and-the-95-theses

https://www.historytoday.com/archive/charles-v%E2%80%99s-spanish-abdication

https://en.wikipedia.org/wiki/Charles_II,_Archduke_of_Austria

http://www.lipizzanconnection.com/history/

http://www.lipizzan.org/aboutlipizzans.html

https://www.tempelfarms.com/the-history-of-the-lipizzan.html

https://dailyhistory.org/What_was_the_role_of_the_Popes_in_the_Renaissance%3F

Horses Arrive in the Americas

Five hundred years ago there were bison, thousands of deer and dogs in North America and llamas in South America. There were no hogs, horses or cattle; these animals had to come from Europe with the early explorers, early settlers and colonists. There are currently over nine million horses in the United States alone. Horses were brought to the Americas, mostly by Europeans, and now the United States alone has more horses than all of Europe; Europe has a little over six million horses.

The common method for loading horses on ships in that era was to blindfold, then hoist them on board by means of a belly sling and a crane. Once on deck and in their stalls, they were again suspended by belly slings for the voyage with their front feet hobbled and just touching the deck then they were tethered by restraining lines to prevent injury. The standard practice with horses was to suspend the animals in these slings, or "horse hammocks", during calm weather and then lower them completely to the deck in rough seas; otherwise they would be mercilessly tossed about if left suspended.

Spanish horse in sling during crossing. Many ships that transported horses had slings to keep horses upright. [110]

When a ship anchored off the coast of the New World, the horses that survived the voyage were brought out of their stalls in the ship's hold. In order to prevent the horses from panicking, they were blindfolded and carefully raised from below deck by hoists attached to slings surrounding the horses' bodies. In these early days before wharves were built, the horses were lowered into the water and made to swim ashore, led by men in row boats.

Christopher Columbus was well received in the court of King Ferdinand and Queen Isabella after his first voyage in 1492. The first horses known to arrive in the New World were transported by Christopher Columbus on his second voyage in 1493. In a letter of

May 23, 1493, to their secretary Fernando de Zafra, Ferdinand and Isabella wrote, "Among the persons which we order to go in the above-mentioned armada we have agreed that twenty lancers are to sail with horses. Five of them shall bring spare horses and those horses shall be mares." The journey was very hard for the horses. There is no record of how many horses actually arrived in the New World. An eyewitness to Christopher Columbus' landing in Puerto Rico said that, "Guacanagari, the friendly local Taino chief, came down to the shore to see the ships. When there, he admired the lofty bulwarks, examined the tackle of the ships, observed attentively the instruments of iron, but fixed his eye most upon the horses of which the Indians had never seen before. A great number of fine horses had been brought out by the Spaniards. These horses had plated bits, trappings of gay colors, and straps highly polished. The appearance of these animals was not without terror to the Indians, for they suspected they fed on human flesh."

Columbus at the court of Ferdinand and Isabella after his first voyage. [111]

By 1494 Columbus was so convinced of the value of horses for military and civilian use that he wrote to the Spanish sovereign requesting that horses be included on all future voyages. His request was favorably received and for several years each fleet's manifest included horses, especially broodmares. Ponce De Leon, Baron de Lery et de St. Just, Hernando Cortes, Lucas Vasques de Ayllón, Pedro de Mendoza, Hernando de Soto, Francisco Vásquez de Coronado and M. L'Escarbot all brought horses to the New World.

Over the next decades, the Spanish, French, Dutch and British all competed for control of the New World. The Spanish established many colonies in southern North America, as well as in Mexico and South America. The English established the first permanent colony in North America at Jamestown. Samuel du Champlain founded Quebec City for the French in 1608, and Holland established a trading outpost in present-day New York City in 1624. Today, there are many breeds of horses in the Americas that are the result of cross breeding of the horses brought by the early settlers and explorers. Importing horses for a purpose and breeding for a purpose did not begin until the Americas were well established. Early settlers to the Americas probably assumed the needs for horses would be the same as they had been in Europe – transportation, warfare and farming. Little did they know that just surviving would be so difficult and that hippophagy (the eating of horse flesh) would be necessary for survival. As situations improved, more horses survived and horses served many purposes. Until the last years of the 18th century, livestock received a significantly low amount of care. Domestic animals could survive only if they were strong enough to last through the winter, relying mainly on forests and natural meadowland for subsistence. Farmers became more attentive to the well-being of their animals when lucrative markets or sporting opportunities could be gained.

The Breeding of Horses in Early America

The first concern for the early settlers was size. In the early Americas many of the horses brought from Europe were small. Settlers soon leaned that a larger, more powerful and more versatile horse was needed. The Dutch horses were over 14 hands and the English horses were under 13 hands; most likely Irish Hobby horses. Stringent regulations were adopted against allowing under size colts and stallions to wander as they pleased. To foster quality in American horses, as early as 1668, the court of Massachusetts decreed that only horses "of comely proportions and 14 hands in stature" could graze on town commons. A law was enacted by William Penn in Pennsylvania in 1687 which set a minimum height of 13 hands for free ranging horses. Any horse more than 18 months old and less than 13 hands had to be gelded. This really did not accomplish what was hoped. It was not until the close of the colonial days when farmers had facilities for breeding stock that there was an increase in the size of the horses.
(cited from: http://www.imh.org/exhibits/online/legacy-of-the-horse/colonial-horses/)

Although there are many breeds of horses in the Americas, the breeds and types listed here are those that developed in early America.

Travel was difficult in early America due to the long distances between towns and the lack of roads so a pacing/ambling horse was the answer. The pacing horses of Rhode Island were sought after for travel by many. The **Narragansett Pacer** made valuable contributions to many horse breeds of North America. The horse is named for the area from which they developed – the Narragansett Bay area of Rhode Island. Their ancestors were probably among the English and Dutch horses which arrived in Massachusetts between 1629 and 1635. The Narragansett Pacer was known as a saddle horse that provided a comfortable ambling gait that was sure-footed; they had great endurance. The Narragansett Pacer was the primary export and chief source of income for the area. It was bred in vast numbers in the 1700s and exported to plantations in Cuba, Barbados and West India Islands to be used on the plantations. This continued into the 18th century. The pacers of Rhode Island were highly desired; so much so that there were continuous raids by Spaniards on the Islands to steal the horses. This seems to indicate that had there been pacing horses among the horses of Spain, the Spanish dependencies would have secured their horses from Spain rather than steal them or go to Rhode Island and pay the high prices that the pacers brought. The breed reigned as the most desirable saddle horse for a century and a half. The breed eventually became extinct as colonial roads improved and people began to drive trotting horses more than ride these ambling, smooth gaited horses.

Narragansett pacer: etching from Frank Forester's Horse and Horsemanship of the United States and British Provinces of North America 1857. [112]

The sturdy qualities of the Narragansett pacers have been perpetuated also by James Fenimore Cooper in his tales of the American wilderness. He seats his heroine, Alice Munro, on a Narragansett Pacer in *The Last of the Mohicans*. The horses were evidently still obtainable in Cooper's day and he must have been an admirer of the breed, for he brings them into his stories frequently. George Washington owned a pair of Narragansett Pacers, which he highly valued. He wrote about racing them in his diary. Esther Forbes, Paul Revere's Pulitzer Prize winning biographer, argues forcibly that the horse that Revere rode from Charlestown to Lexington was a Narragansett Pacer but this has been debated. *(cited from: http://www.newenglandhistoricalsociety. com/narragansett-pacer-lost-horse-new-england-colonies/ and https://archive.org/stream/ horseraisinginco00phil/horseraisinginco00phil_djvu.txt)*

The **Conestoga Horse** was developed in the United States during the 18th and early 19th centuries for pulling the famous Conestoga wagons that were produced in Lancaster County, Pennsylvania. The Conestoga Valley was settled in the early 18th century. It was then wilderness but a country of unsurpassed fertility. Its first homemakers were farmers. They came from the upper Rhine country and Switzerland. With them came a good number of French Huguenots. These people needed horses for many things, all of which were hard work. These horses were not bred by any scientific system but by a process of natural selection. As generation succeeded generation a horse evolved that met the demands placed upon it by understanding owners. As settlers began heading west from Pennsylvania, more and more horses were needed to pull their heavy wagons. The Conestoga wagon was designed to meet this need, and the Conestoga horse was called upon to power it. In hauling these wagons over the Allegheny Mountains the Conestoga won its place in the story of American transportation. It is thought that horses owned by George Washington may have been used for breeding in the development of Conestoga horses. *(cited from: http://articles.mcall.com/1988-03-06/ entertainment/2614046_1_five-horses-conestoga-breed)*

Conestoga Horse, engraving from the Report of the Commissioner of Agriculture for the year 1863. [113]

Conestoga Wagon 1883. [114]

112

The Morgan Horse is one of the earliest horse breeds developed in the United States tracing back to the foundation sire, Figure, born in 1789. The horse was later named Justin Morgan after his owner. Morgans served many roles in early American history, being used as farm horses, driving horses, for harness racing, as well as general riding animals and as cavalry horses during the American Civil War on both sides of the conflict. Morgans have influenced other major American breeds, including the American Saddlebred, American Quarter Horse, Tennessee Walking Horse and the Standardbred. Justin Morgan also proved to be one of the greatest breeding horses of all time. As the saga of the little stallion grew, countless mares were bred to him. So prepotent were the genes of this stallion that no matter what type of mare he was bred to, be the mare of heavy draft or refined racing-type, his offspring inherited his image and abilities. While most breeds develop by breeding horses of similar characteristics to each other, Justin Morgan's ability to pass his characteristics to his offspring for generations to come allowed this single stallion to found an entire breed in his likeness. Today, every registered Morgan traces back to Justin Morgan through his best-known sons Bulrush, Sherman and Woodbury. *(cited from: https://en.wikipedia.org/wiki/Morgan_horse and http://afs.okstate.edu/breeds/horses/morgan/index.html)*

Statue of Justin Morgan in Vermont (home of the Morgan horse) Dedicated in 1921 at UVM.
115

(For more information about the many horse breeds of the Americas, be sure to read: *Horses of the Americas: From the prehistoric horse to modern American breeds.* by Gloria Austin)

Breeding Horses During the Industrial and Technical Revolutions 1750-1920

The American Revolution and the Civil War resulted in dramatic changes in America - and around the world as well. In addition, many inventions began to "revolutionize" the way people lived. The first wave of the Industrial Revolution lasted from the late 1700s to the mid-1800s. The next wave took place from the mid-1800s to the early 1900s and is often called the Technical Revolution. During the second phase, large factories and companies began to use more technologies to mass produce goods. But this was not the end of the era of the horse. Horses were incredibly important in these new large, industrialized cities.

The standard of living for many people improved during the Industrial Revolution even though wages for people who worked in factories were low and working conditions could be dangerous. Many children worked in the factories too. Cities soon became overcrowded because people from the countryside moved to cities for jobs. The Industrial Revolution spread around the world and by the 1900s the United States had become the world's leading industrial nation.

Horses in the The American Revolution

At the outbreak of the Revolutionary War, most of the British troops in the American colonies were billeted in Boston. There was no cavalry, few field guns and no field supply system. The shortage of cavalry in the Revolutionary War was a major drawback for the British. In October 1775, the British undertook a remarkable effort to supply the army in Boston with enough quality fresh

The British evacuate Boston, March 17, 1776. [116]

provisions to last through the winter. The firm of Mure, Son & Atkinson was contracted to furnish enough fresh food and livestock to fill 36 ships. Only 13 ships eventually made it to Boston. Only the preserved food (sauerkraut, vinegar, and porter, a type of beer) survived intact. Most of the other provisions were rotten or damaged. Out of 856 horses shipped, only 532 survived the voyage. Shipment of many commodities from Britain was deemed impracticable so the army resorted to local sources for fresh food, fodder and transportation. This had a great impact on the course of the war; when supply reserves dropped below the two month level, which they often did, British generals stopped thinking about offensive action and began to plan evacuation. To have any hope of victory, the British had to seek out the rebel army and defeat it. Yet far too often their soldiers were forced to sit and wait or, worse, to evacuate a position, garrison, or city that had already been gained through difficult fighting. The effect that logistics deficiencies had on these decisions to wait or pull back is undeniable. The convoy of 36 ships marked the last time that Britain attempted to ship fresh food and livestock to its army. When the British were forced to evacuate Boston, the whole complexion of the war changed. No longer a static siege, General Washington realized that cavalry would be useful in patrolling the Atlantic coast line for possible British landings and to serve as couriers. The speed of the horse made it valuable in delivering messages to political leaders and generals. Long before telegraph, telephone and the internet, the horse was the fastest way to deliver a message. At a canter a horse could travel up to 25-30 mph for short distances and trot up to 8-12 mph over a sustained period. Horses also hauled supplies and armaments. The value of a horse was so high, that it was a capital offense to steal one. *(cited from: http://www.almc.army.mil/alog/issues/sepoct99/ms409.htm)*

The horse was a key factor in the winning of the Revolution fought in the geographic vastness of the Colonial America. Despite occupying every major city, the British remained at a disadvantage in the countryside where the use of the horse proved to be a critical element for transport and communication. The kind of warfare employed by the colonists required swift pursuit and withdrawal; it was a type of guerrilla warfare learned by the colonists in the French and Indian War. The horse was the deciding factor in these types of tactics used to defeat a better organized yet less adaptable enemy.

Horses and the Expansion of the American West

After the American Revolution, postwar economic conditions in the east were bad therefore, westward expansion gained momentum. The Northwest Ordinance, passed by Congress in 1787, further spurred westward immigration. Slowly the map of a continent spanning nation was forming.

Slowly the continent spanning nation was forming. [117]

In 1804 Meriwether Lewis and William Clark led a party across the wilderness acquired by the Louisiana Purchase and through the Oregon Country. Once beyond

115

the Great Falls of the Missouri, Lewis became increasingly aware that horses would be the only means of fighting against time and geography since winter was coming. In their journeys they met Toussaint Charbonneau and his Indian wife, Sacagawea. Through Sacagawea, they were able to acquire horses from her brother who also provided information about the trails to the west. Without the horses the journey could not have continued. During their 7,689 mile, 28 month journey, they made the first U.S. crossing from the Missouri River to the Pacific coast. Their expedition bolstered the U.S. claim to the Oregon Territory which America acquired with the Oregon Treaty of 1846. The expedition of Lewis and Clark impacted America's imagination and desire to start a new life in the west.

Mountain men and trappers and explorers roamed the North American Rocky Mountains from about 1810 through the 1880s with a peak population in the early 1840s. These trail blazers and mountain men led the way for covered wagons. They were instrumental in opening up the various trails that eventually widened into wagon roads allowing Americans in the east to settle the new territories of the far west. The mountain men and the big fur companies originally opened these routes to serve the mule train based inland fur trade. Eventually organized wagon trains of settlers ventured over these roads to settle the American West.

Many of the new settlers in the west were farmers. Technology had to be improved so that agricultural equipment could be more cost effective; up to three horses or six oxen were needed to counter the immense friction of poor plow designs. In July of 1831 twenty two-year-old Cyrus McCormick cut six acres of grain in one afternoon with his reaper. Previous to this it took two to three men an entire day to hand scythe the quantity of grain that a reaper could cut in a few hours.

The original McCormick Reaper as invented in 1831. McCormick's invention gave the farmer an extra power source – the horse. [118]

On January 24, 1848 - only nine days before California was added to the American republic - gold was discovered in California. Thousands of people headed for California. Few discovered gold but they stayed to farm or start businesses. Cites grew along the route to California too and more states entered the union. This encouraged the growth of stagecoach and wagon transportation. The most common starting point for the journey west was Independence, Missouri. The journey usually began in late April or early

May. Often times there were huge jam ups, as everyone wanted to leave at the same time. Often wagons were overloaded and the trails were littered with debris. At first there were tent cities and, as cities and towns developed, the horse was used for the building of the towns.

As the West developed, people began to travel from town to town. Stagecoaches provided regular transportation and communication between St. Louis and San Francisco. The Butterfield Overland Mail received the first contract by the U.S. Postmaster in 1857 and stages began running in 1858 and ran through 1861. It carried passengers and U.S. Mail from Memphis, Tennessee and St. Louis, Missouri to San Francisco, California. The Stagecoach was pulled by a team of six horses that were changed out every ten miles. The driver drove a route that was fifty to sixty miles long. The stage traveled day and night and made periodic stopovers at home stations where passengers were fed and sometimes spent the night.

Horses and mules were used to get supplies to the towns in large freight wagons. [119]

As cities and towns developed, there was a need for timely communication between the settlements. The Pony Express operated for a short time from April 3, 1860 to October 24, 1861. The purpose was to provide a faster mail delivery service between St. Joseph, Missouri and Sacramento, California. Most riders were around twenty years old; the youngest was eleven. The oldest was forty. Approximately one hundred eighty-three men rode for The Pony Express. Four hundred horses were purchased to stock the express route. The average horse was a little over fourteen hands and weighed nine hundred pounds. Riders rode one horse for ten to fifteen miles, and then changed out for a fresh mount. Each rider rode about a seventy-five to one hundred mile stretch until relieved by a new rider. Overall, the route was around two thousand miles, and took about ten days.

"Frank E. Webner, Pony Express Rider, circa 1861," House Divided: The Civil War Research Engine at Dickinson College [120]

The Pony Express prompted the idea of building a transcontinental railroad.

The building of the railroads was one of the biggest engineering feats of the nineteenth century. At any one time ten thousand animals and eight thousand men were working on the construction. The growth of the railroads brought more people; more people needed more horses. Horses were needed for transportation and farming and building the railroads.

Horse breeding at this point in history was not so much about the "breed" of the horse but rather about the utilitarian purpose of the horse. Horses and mules were needed more than ever. The new farming tools along with the creation of larger farms and the expansion of railroads and canals for easier shipment influenced an agricultural expansion that led to the need for more horses and mules. Mules became incredibly useful and America became famous for their amazing mules. The national census of mules in the U.S. in 1860 was 1,139,553. Between 1867 and 1869, the horse population increased by thirty seven percent and mule population by thirty two percent. Between 1900-1910, national horse population increased by seventy percent from thirteen million to twenty-three million.

(cited from: https://www.ducksters.com/history/us_1800s/industrial_revolution.php, http://www.bl.uk/learning/timeline/item107855.html, https://www.history.com/topics/inventions/cotton-gin-and-eli-whitney, http://www.newlanark.org/learningzone/clitp-ageofinvention.php, http://www.saburchill.com/history/chapters/IR/036.html, https://www.asme.org/engineering-topics/articles/transportation/robert-fulton, https://www.history.com/topics/industrial-revolution/industrial-revolution, https://www.wired.com/2008/09/sept-18-1830-horse-beats-iron-horse-for-the-time-being/https://home.bt.com/tech-gadgets/internet/the-ss-great-eastern-and-the-amazing-story-of-the-transatlantic-telegraph-cable-11363992848355, https://www.smithsonianmag.com/travel/how-charles-dickens-saw-london-13198155/, https://www.farmcollector.com/farm-life/making-american-plow, http://www.lewis-clark.org/article/3342, https://truewestmagazine.com/the-mormon-handcart-migration/, https://www.farmcollector.com/farm-life/making-american-plow , http://www.historynet.com/mormon-handcart-horrors.htm, http://kentuckyancestors.org/the-untraveled-history-of-the-wilderness-road/, http://www.wondersandmarvels.com/2015/09/why-i-fell-in-love-with-sarah-royce-pioneer-woman-of-the-gold-rush.html, https://nationalponyexpress.org/historic-pony-express-trail/founders/, http://amhistory.si.edu/ourstory/activities/sodhouse/more.html, http://www.lrgaf.org/articles/ahta.htm, http://plainshumanities.unl.edu/encyclopedia/doc/egp.gen.040)

To learn more about Horses in America be sure to read: The American Horse by Gloria Austin, For more information about the westward expansion of the United States be sure to read: Westward Ho: Concord Coach - Staging and Freighting by Gloria Austin and to learn more about Mules be sure to read: The Mighty Mule by Gloria Austin)

Horses in the American Civil War

The new country was not without growing pains. As the country began to grow, the states in the south started to worry that the states would lose the power to make laws for their own state. Many northern states had outlawed slavery and the South was worried that the United States would outlaw slavery in all the states. So, the South separated from the Union. The war was fought from 1861 until 1865 when the North triumphed and the United States were once again united. The Civil War was the bloodiest war ever fought in the history of the United States. An average of six hundred men died every day during the war. It was the greatest single event in the nineteenth century that called for massive mobilization of horses to make use of their ability to perform work.

Horses were one of the biggest expenditures of the war budget. The purchase of the horse was only part of the expense. The horses also needed training, feed, shoes, proper fitting tack and veterinary care. By 1864 a good cavalry horse cost three thousand dollars; that would be equal to about forty-eight thousand dollars today. Civil War horses and mules primarily served in three sectors: artillery, cavalry and supply.

At the start of the Civil War, the Northern states held approximately three and a half million horses, while there were about one and a half million in the Confederate states. The border states of Missouri and Kentucky had an additional eight hundred thousand horses. In addition, there were one hundred thousand mules in the North, eight hundred thousand in the seceding states and two hundred thousand in Kentucky and Missouri. Throughout the course of the war, horses and mules perished at rates as astonishing as the human death toll. Historians estimate one and a half million horses and mules died during their wartime service. An estimated three million equines participated in the war effort, a figure thirty six percent greater than the number of soldiers populating the northern and southern armies. Approximately fifty percent of the mules and horses drafted into the war did not survive. Horses died in great numbers from disease and exhaustion and made for large targets on the battlefield.

Soldiers preferred to shoot horses rather than the enemy, because by removing the horse, the cavalry couldn't advance and artillery and much needed supplies couldn't be hauled.

Lacking a strong cavalry tradition, the Union was outmatched in the first two years of the war by the Confederacy's equestrian military units, which effectively and creatively mobilized their horses' speed to scout and attack supply trains. The majority of Civil War battles were fought in the South and it resulted in the confiscation of horses, mules and donkeys from Southern farmers who relied on the equines for their livelihood. The once vast supply of horses in the United States was greatly diminished by late 1863, causing a single horse to be considered more valuable than a soldier. While men were still plentiful in the North, attrition had decimated its horse population. The Shenandoah Valley Campaigns of 1864 placed an additional strain on an already depleted supply of horses. General Phil Sheridan, for example, required one hundred fifty mounts per day during his chapter in the campaign alone. By 1864 the Union Army relied heavily on prized horses in the South to replace the five hundred horses it needed daily to sustain its army in the field.

Union army wagon train halted and guarded from Confederate cavalry near Brandy Station, VA, in May 1863. [121]

In the South, horses were signs of elite power, whereas in the North, they were more utilitarian, bred to work, not to race or ride to oversee the plantation. The Southern cavalry was a rich man's undertaking. The Union often purchased Morgans, a uniquely American breed known for endurance, versatility, heart and courage. Most importantly, more than a breed, the Quartermaster Manual had explicit features that were deemed necessary for a desirable type and temperament of mules and horses. The manual stated "Horses for cavalry must be sound in all respects, and free from vice or blemish; not less than fifteen hands high, and not less than five, or more than nine years old, and of dark colors; (horses between nine and ten yeas of age, if still vigorous, sprightly, and healthy may be accepted;) surefooted; free in their movements; good sight; full firm chest; good disposition, with boldness and courage, and with more bottom than spirit."

After the war many soldiers returned to their farms only to find them overrun by trees and brush caused by neglect or abandonment. Their horses and mules had been requisitioned by a nearby army for the war effort. Some veterans arrived at their homestead only to receive the news that their former livelihoods of farms and fields had been sold by wives and family members to purchase necessities. In the absence of husbands, fathers and brothers, many wives and children tried to keep the farms working but usually with little success. *(cited from: http://ushistoryscene.com/article/civilwaranimals/, http://www.thomaslegion.net/americancivilwar/totalcivilwarhorseskilled.html, http://www.civilwar.com/overview/315-weapons/148532-cavalry-62478.html, https://civilwar.mrdonn.org/supplytrains.html, https://www.civilwarhorses.net/links.php?326695, http://www.civil-war.net/cw_images/files/images/367.jpg, http://www.loc.gov/teachers/classroommaterials/presentationsandactivities/presentations/timeline/riseind/city, https://www.earthintransition.org/2013/02/horses-in-the-civil-war/, https://www.youtube.com/watch?v=qLbVPjxqlZ0 11th Ohio Volunteer Cavalry)*

This was the home of Lydia Leister. Her home was used as the headquarters for Union Major General George G. Meade during the Battle of Gettysburg. Lydia returned to her home after the battle to find her home punctured by numerous gunshot holes and seventeen dead horses in her yard, several of which had been burned around her best peach tree, killing it. Her cow and horse were gone, her apple trees were destroyed, two tons of hay was gone from the barn, her wheat had been trampled, her spring spoiled by the dead horses and all her fence rails burned. [122]

Horses and the Growth of Cities

Between 1880 and 1900, cities in the United States grew at a dramatic rate. Owing most of their population growth to the expansion of industry, U.S. cities grew by about fifteen million people in the two decades before 1900. Many of those who helped account for the population growth of cities were immigrants arriving from around the world. A steady stream of people from rural America also migrated

121

to the cities during this period. Between 1880 and 1890, almost forty percent of the townships in the United States lost population because of migration. Industrial expansion and population growth radically changed the face of the nation's cities.

American horse population peaked at twenty five million in 1915. The mule population reached the peak of six million in 1925; with mules being used primarily in the south.

In 1775 James Watt patented the steam engine, a machine that would become a symbol of the industrial revolution. After refining the steam engine, James Watt invented a standard measure of mechanical work – thirty three thousand foot-pounds of work per minute, or one horsepower. This unit allowed customers to estimate how many horses an engine could replace and to gauge whether replacing their horses would be economical. In many cases, it wasn't. For much of the 19th century, horses were the engine of choice for applications that required flexibility or mobility and for businesses that could not afford a large capital outlay. They were hooked up to engines through circular sweeps, rotating platforms and treadmills and harnessed to vehicles on wheels and tracks.

In the cities, the horse was indispensable for the movement of people and freight. The commerce and transportation of modern cities initially relied on the horse. A city powered by horses needed shelters for them to rest and sleep. In just New York City, there were over four thousand stables by the beginning of the 20th century - some five stories high. Where did people in the cities get their horses and carriages? The Van Tassell and Kearney Horse Auction Mart was one option in New York City. Formed as a general auction house in the 1870s, the company began specializing in show horses and fine carriages for the city's elite, operating several equine auction buildings along East 13th Street.

The most common form of transportation within cities was the horse railway (omnibus/trolley). By 1886 there were over five hundred railways in three hundred cities in the U.S.; a generation had adapted to their use and urban development patterns began to change.

Instead of having to find housing in dark and dingy tenements next to a factory, a workman could commute on a horsecar and railway system which allowed a growing dispersion and separation of residential from commercial land uses. Local merchants usually had a big increase in trade after the start of a new horsecar line on the street in front of their establishments. Horses were vital when it came to ground transport within the city. City horses hauled everything from steel to home delivery of milk. They powered ferries and pulled trolleys. Goods from the expanded railway and steamboat lines could only be distributed to their final destinations under the power of horses, which meant that horse-drawn transport grew more efficient in parallel with steam technology.

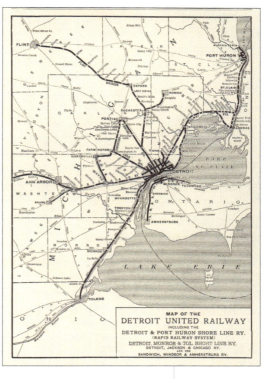

Map of the Detroit United Railway including the Detroit & Port Huron Shore Line. [123]

The horses were in turn, dependent on a vast complex of human resources. Teamsters, hostlers, grooms, farriers, blacksmiths, veterinarians, wheelwrights, carriage builders, draymen, liverymen, makers of saddles, harnesses, whips and other horse accouterments as well as manure transporters and rendering workers were all needed to keep the cities moving. In addition, hay and oats were raised in a grain belt surrounding each city. The horse trade itself moved thousands of horses from the farms where they were raised; roughly one tenth were sent to cities with the rest going to industrial or other users.

Innovations in breeding produced larger and larger horses; these industrial-strength horses could pull even larger loads especially after the development of vehicles made with modern materials. For instance, the Detroit Fire Department specified sizes for the various apparatus: one thousand one hundred pounds for hose wagon teams, one thousand four hundred pounds for steamer teams and one thousand seven hundred pounds for hook and ladder teams. Realizing that the framers were the ones breeding horses, the USDA took up the improvement of horse breeding in earnest by joining with breed associations in offering prize money at local fairs. In 1862 the Morrill Act gave states public lands provided the lands be sold or used for profit and the proceeds used to establish at least one college—hence, land grant colleges—that would teach agriculture and the mechanical arts. Colleges of veterinary medicine began their affiliation with land grant universities in 1879 with the opening of the veterinary college at Iowa State University. Today, of the thirty veterinary colleges only two—those at the University of Pennsylvania and at Tufts University—are not affiliated with land grant schools.

Draft horse breeding programs in Canada flourished during the late 19th and early 20th centuries in response to the agricultural sector's demand for more horsepower. Photo courtesy of the Provincial Archives of Alberta. [124]

Horses in World War I

When the war began, the British army had a mere twenty five thousand horses. That may seem like a lot of horses but, considering that eight million horses and countless mules and donkeys died in the war, it then seems hard to imagine how the various nations were able to obtain so many horses and mules. Horses were shipped from Spain, Portugal, New Zealand, South Africa, India, Canada, and America.

To accommodate the rapidly increasing needs of the army, there were eventually 33 auxiliary remount depots established, plus two animal embarkation depots including Newport News, RH. [125]

At one-point America was sending one thousand horses a day to Europe. Beginning in late November 1914, the port of Newport News, Virginia became the biggest shipper of American war horses and mules to the British army in Europe in a crucial effort that helped the Allies win the war. Killing American horses and mules became a strategic priority for the Germans. A German sabotage campaign was the first attempt at using germs in warfare. Clandestine attempts by German agents to infect and kill the horses were not even discovered until after the war. At the outbreak of the war, Americans owned between twenty four and twenty five million horses and four and a half million mules. There were two million horses in the United Kingdom, a little over three million in France, one million in Italy, four and a half million in Germany and almost two million in Austria. More than half the horses on earth lived in the United States and Russia. *(from US Department of Agriculture Yearbook 1920 pp. 701-717, table 229)* The U. S continued to have a robust horse and mule population throughout the war years due to the Federal Government encouraging peak production of foodstuffs with the "Food Will Win the War" slogan.

Captain Sidney Galtery, an English Remount Officer, had the job of supervising the handling of horses in France from their arrival on ships through the casting of horses. His book. *"The Horse and the War,"* is a detailed accounting of the War Horse in World War I. He commented on the American horses that were shipped to Europe that "… of all the breeds and cross-breeds of horses in the world the one from the United States and Canada has proved paramount and incomparably the best…. Hardiness, placidity of temper, strength, and power, virility of constitution, with what is called 'good heart,' versatility and extraordinary activity for his size and weight — these are characteristics that have impressed themselves for all time on all who have had to do with him… the light draught of American origin has come to stay in this country. After all, they are a distinct type. Some may be better than others, and some may be heavier in physique than the vast majority, but these latter are as if they had all come out of the same mold. By comparison, the British light draught is a nondescript, a misfit. He could be anything — a half-bred Shire or Clydesdale, a Welsh cob, a heavy-ish Hackney, a Cleveland bay, or a heavy-weight 'hunter' without true hunter lines and action. All these odds and ends of horse-flesh we have seen pass through remount depots on route to the theatres of war. They were classed as light draught because they were neither heavy draught nor a riding horse. But the Yankee was essentially and absolutely a light draught horse, true to type, varying not at all in character and very little in the non-essential details. He is the real equine hero of the war, and by his triumphs, which must be as real in peacetime as in war, he simply must take his place, and an important one, too, in the horse population of these Islands."

Breeding Horses in Modern Times 1920 - Present

On the Move Without Horses

North Americans employed four million horses in 1840 for agricultural work and travel. By 1900 they were harnessing more than twenty four million (a six-fold increase) to plow fields, as well as pull street trolleys, drays, brewery wagons, city vehicles, omnibuses, and carriages. For every three people there trod one working horse in the U.S. There are now 1.3 people for every car in the U.S. By 1890 New Yorkers took an average of two hundred ninety seventy horse-car rides per person a year. Today, they hail an average of one hundred cab rides. In a New York City traffic study undertaken in 1907, horse-drawn vehicles moved at an average speed of 11.5 mph. A similar study conducted almost sixty years later found that automobiles moved through the city's business district at an average speed of only 8.5 mph.

New York, 5th Ave. - 1900 more horses than cars. [126]

Many of the new technologies developed during World War I eliminated the need for horses. The internal combustion engine took from the horse the distinction it had enjoyed over the centuries as the sole, or primary, source of mobile energy and swept the horses from the road, the farm and the battlefield. But it took the automobile and tractor nearly fifty years to dislodge the horse from farms, public transport and wagon delivery systems throughout North America. Not only were horse's jobs gone but gone too were the jobs of all those involved with the horse economy; the teamsters, the hostlers, the grooms, the farriers, wheelwrights, carriage painters, carriage builders, draymen, liverymen, makers of saddles, whips, blankets and other horse clothing, manure transporters – all no longer necessary. Gone too were the jobs of the farmers in the belt of farms around each city, growing the forage to feed the city horses, the

New York, 5th Ave. - 1913 more cars than horses. [127]

hay and grain dealers. The "job" of the horse became one of companion and teammate in athletic endeavors; hopefully to never again have to endure the horrors of war on such a large scale. *(cited from: "Where Have All the Horse Gone?", pp 185-86, back cover and pictures below cited from: https://medium.com/@alearningaday/horses-cars-and-the-disruptive-decade-358b3fd6fdb9)*

Purposeful Breeding in Modern Times

According to the American Horse Council 2017 Economic Impact Study, the equine industry in the U.S. generates approximately $122 billion in total economic impact, an increase from $102 billion in the 2005 Economic Impact Study. The industry also provides a total employment impact of 1.74 million, and generates $79 billion in total salaries, wages, and benefits. The current number of horses in the United States stands at 7.2 million. Texas, California, and Florida continue to be the top 3 states with the highest population of horses. 38 million, or 30.5%, of U.S. households contain a horse enthusiast, and 38% of participants are under the age of 18. Additionally, approximately 80 million acres of land is reserved for horse-related activities. *(cited from: http://www.horsecouncil.org/press-release/ahcf-announces-results-2017-economic-impact-study/)*

If horses are not being used for farming or transportation or industry, what are all of the horses doing? Shortly after World War I, it didn't take long for people to miss the horses. Movies and television romanticized horses and created plenty of horse "stars". Horse crazed children imagined themselves owning a horse and "saving the day" on the back of a horse or riding into the sunset on a horse; soon many horse toys and products flooded the market.

Horses in America today are used for both recreational and commercial purposes. Out of the grand total of 7.2 million horses, 3.91 million are used for recreational purposes, 2.72 million for showing, 1.75 million for other activities including farm work, rodeo, polo, police work etc. and 840,000 are used for racing.

Horses are purposefully bred for each of these purposes. There are many breeds of horses and each breed has a specific conformation. The conformation (form) of the horse helps to determine the purpose (function) that best suits the horse. To understand how horses are purposefully bred, it is important to have a knowledge of form to function through the understanding of bio-mechanics.

Chapter 3 - Understanding Purposeful Breeding in Modern Times

Basic Equine Biomechanics

The definition of conformation can be articulated in different ways. Webster's Dictionary simply defines it as the "form or outline of an animal." This can be applied to the standard diagrams of a horse from a lateral, cranial, and plantar view with plumb lines applied. This procedure establishes a basic visual means to determine if the limbs are straight and the angles are correct. Another definition of conformation is "the symmetrical arrangements of its parts." This encompasses the horseman's perception of the "well-made" horse. Those parameters are often described as beauty, balance and symmetry. The third and most significant definition is the "relationship of form and function". This is the way that the horse's structure allows it to perform its method of ambulation either on its own or while working or performing for man.

Conformation becomes the common denominator to the horse's ability to perform and stay sound. The correlation of the three factors (standard of excellence, dynamics of locomotion, and soundness) provides a method to better understand the meaning of the conformation relationship of form to function. For instance, the location of the center of gravity of a horse is helpful in understanding why 60% – 65% of the horse's body weight is born by the forelimbs.

The evaluation of conformation has been and is currently subjective; however, more and more objective evaluations of conformation are being developed with the advent of sophisticated research enhanced by the application of modalities. These modalities provide specific information as to the movement of the horse and define the effects of conformation on the movement of specific parts of the horse. The evaluation of conformation can be divided by examining the following:

1. Head, neck, body and balance
2. Forelimb (from the top of the scapula to the bottom of the foot)
3. Hindlimb (from the top of the croup to the bottom of the foot)
4. Type
5. Way of going

(*cited from: https://aaep.org/sites/default/files/issues/proceedings-08proceedings-z9100108000001.PDF*)

In order to evaluate the conformation of a horse, and thus purposeful breeding, we need to have a basic understanding of horse anatomy.

The Equine Skeleton

The skeleton gives support for the muscles, protection for the internal organs, and possesses the necessary mobility of its parts for the horse to move at various speeds or lie down or graze.

Perhaps the best way to explain an equine skeleton is to compare it to that of a human. Horses and humans have many similar, comparative and associated parts with similar functions. The legs of the horse however, are the most misunderstood when comparing to a that of a human. The horse possesses no collar-bone, consequently there is no bony connection between his fore extremity and trunk. The humerus, elbow, and fore-arm are the same in both, except that the ulna is complete in the horse, only in very rare instances. The knee (carpal bones) of the horse corresponds to the wrist of man. The five bones between our wrist and the first row of knuckles are represented in the horse by the cannon and splint bones. His fetlock is analogous to the first row of knuckles of our hand (the fetlock joint consists of the distal end of the cannon bone, the long pastern and the two proximal sesamoid bones). The long pastern bone corresponds to the first bone of our middle finger; the short one, to the second bone; the pedal bone, to the third bone; and the hoof, to its nail.

Bones shared by horses and humans. [128]

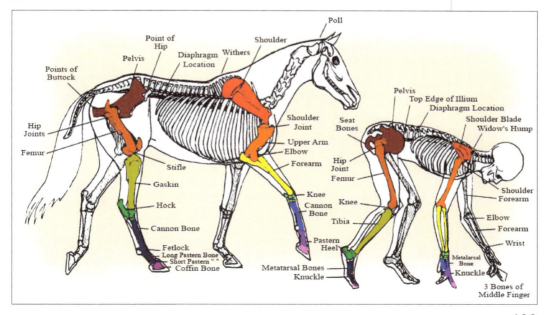

The navicular bone has no counterpart in our frame. In the hind limb, the stifle represents our knee; the tibia, the shin; the hock (tarsal bones), the ankle; the point of the hock, the heel. Thus the horse is an animal which moves on the tips of his fingers and toes and that he has only one complete and functional toe (or finger) to each leg.

With this knowledge we can compare the horse and human skeletons in relation to locomotion.

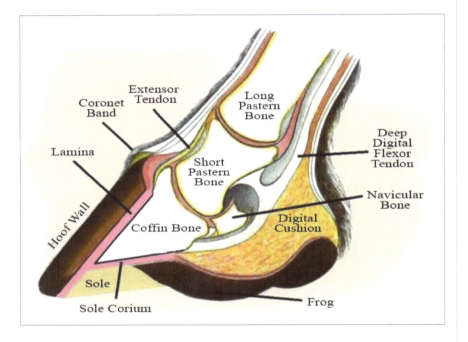

Hoof bone and structure anatomy. [128.]

The skeleton of the horse is not completely developed until age 6. However, horses appear to mature far earlier; for instance a foal can stand within a half hour of its birth. Horses often look more mature than their bones can support; it makes it extra important for riders and trainers to keep the rate of growth plate fusion in mind as they increase work and expectations. This great graphic Stages Of Equine Development, is a good illustration of how long it takes for a horse to become fully mature. *(cited from: https://equineink.com/2019/08/10/the-stages-of-equine-skeletal-development/?fbclid=IwAR3qZBfq739wjMJCzW22GA9tzCmHRTN8h afK56rdYFlzt4pDaxcExlEhqfs)*

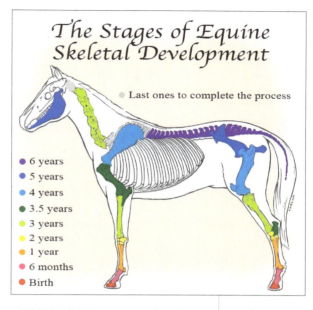

It takes 6 years for a horse's skeletal system to fully mature. 130

Beyond the Bones

Cartilage cushions the joints but they do not always hold them together. That is the job of ligaments. Ligaments are tough fibrous tissue connecting bone to bone. Ligaments are very tough and have very little blood supply. That's why a ligament injury, say in the stifle, is so serious. It takes much longer for ligaments to heal than muscle or bone injuries due to the lack of blood supply. The ligaments have a very serious job to do. They have to keep the bones in place. Often the ligaments have to keep two bones together so that there is virtually no movement in the joint. Take the horse's pelvis for example. The pubic region is where the two halves of his pelvis meet. The ligaments hold this area together which allows the horse to push himself forward with

Ligaments and Tendons of the horse's forelimb and hindlimb. 131

131

his hind legs. If he were to fall on ice and tear these ligaments, he would have great difficulty standing or walking. Ligaments have a lot of responsibility. They have to hold bones together and restrict movement so that joints aren't over extended. So how does all this boney mass move? That's the job of the muscles. They are the brawn of the body. Muscles are really quite dumb. Without the nervous system they wouldn't do anything at all. Nerve impulses cause muscles to contract, moving the bones so that we can run and our horse's can jump. Muscles are attached to bones by tendons, fibrous tissue going from muscle to bone. Coordinating muscular contraction is the job of the brain and nervous system. If you had to think about all the muscles that go into standing up from a chair you probably would never get up. Your nervous system does this for you all the time without you ever having to think about it. This is also true for the horse. *(cited from: https://murdochmethod.com/comparable-parts-you-are-more-like-your-horse-than-you-think/)*

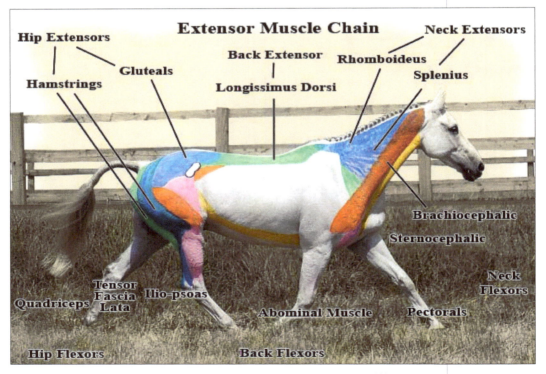

Extensor Muscle Chain of the horse by Gillian Higgins. [132]

Basic Conformation Proportions

Good conformation is key to the intended performance of a horse. Horses with poor conformation may be at higher risk of injury, harder training and lameness. The basic conformation rules allow help to determine a horse's athletic ability for a certain performance.

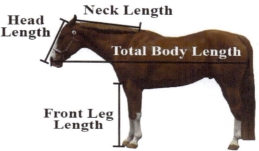

Conformation - Head. [133]

Head
Generally, a horse's neck should be one and a half times the length of the head, where:

- Head length is measured from the front of the muzzle to the top of the poll
- Neck length is measured from the poll to the mid-shoulder

Having these traits provides a balanced head and neck. Too big of a head will cause the horse to be clumsy and move heavy on their front. Too small of a head will cause the horse to lack counterbalance and lose suppleness and action in their front.

Look for the following when evaluating a horse's head:
- Bright, bold, wide set eyes
- Ears set slightly below the poll
- A lower jaw that is clearly defined and well separated underneath the jaw
- Large nostrils
- A clean throatlatch without heavy fat and muscling

Neck
Neck length should be one third of the horse's total body length and equal the length of the horse's front leg. The head should meet the neck at an angle so the horse can flex at the poll and move in balance. The neck should tie into the horse's body fairly high with a distinct chest area below. The base of the neck should be level with the point of the horse's shoulder. This allows the horse to be more flexible, balanced and collect more naturally.

133

Shoulders

When a horse stands square, they should have a shoulder angle between 40 and 55 degrees. At this angle, the horse's elbow is directly below the front of the withers. The elbow should be parallel to the horse's body. Horses with straighter shoulders and pastern angles tend to have shorter strides.

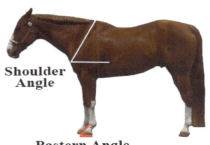

Conformation - Shoulders. 133

Body

A balanced and proportionate body is key to proper leg structure. A proportionate horse is usually square. Square means the height from the withers to ground should equal the length of body (point of shoulder to the point of the buttocks). A proportionate horse will be symmetrical on both sides of its body. Faults in conformation should be symmetrical. Lack of symmetry will stress those points and may harm or limit the horse's ability to perform with grace and ease. Divide the horse into three parts: Chest, Back and Hindquarters (Croup: from point of hip to point of buttock and Quarters: below the croup)

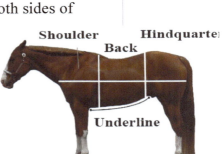

Conformation - Body. 133

Chest

A wide chest (from the front) allows for good stamina, endurance and lung capacity. Good chest and rib form leads to strong leg, shoulder and neck attachment, which creates a powerful athletic performer. Horses can have seventeen to nineteen pairs of ribs except Thoroughbreds and Arabians. Most horses have eighteen pairs. Extra ribs allow for a shorter back, which results in stronger "coupling" of the loin area. The underline of the horse should gradually rise to the hindquarters. Horses that have "spring of rib":

- Have ribs that project outward.
- Have large spaces between the ribs.
- Are shorter backed.
- Have a strong loin.

Back
The back transfers the force and driving power from the hind legs. A horse should have well-formed withers where the shoulder can attach to the rest of the body. The back should be one-third of the horse's length. Measure back length from the middle of the withers to the point of hip. A horse's back should be shorter than their underline. A horse can best move if it has a long neck and short back. A short back also provides more strength for carrying a rider

Hindquarters
A long hindquarter allows for increased range of extension and flexion. A shorter hindquarter supports power and strength. You can think of this by comparing a Warmblood to a Quarter Horse.

> Croup: The croup helps transfer energy for thrust and power from the hindquarters. The croup should be the same height as the withers to maintain balance in the horse's body. It should be round with muscle to provide a smooth contoured shape.
> Quarters: The quarters shouldn't be too sloped or flat. You can measure the quarter length from the point of the horse's hip to the point of buttock. This length should be about 1/3 of the body length.
> Gaskin and Thigh: power running, jumping and other forward movements.

Muscle in the hindquarters must be symmetrical and balanced with the rest of the body. The hindquarters influence the horse's capacity for:

- Speed
- Propelling power
- Strength for collecting

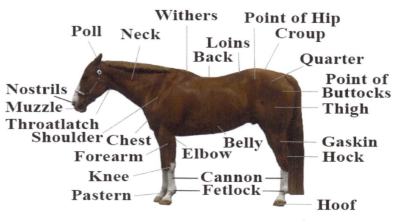

Conformation - Parts of the horse.. [133]

Legs
Hind Legs: The hind legs have fewer lameness issues than the front legs because they only carry 40% of the horse's weight. The front versus rear leg lameness tends to relate to overall horse use. From the rear view, you should be able to draw straight lines down the rear legs. This line should run from the point of the buttock to slightly inside the hock, to the middle of the hoof.

> Hock: The connection from the hindquarter to the gaskin through to the hock is key to hind leg structure. A strong, well-placed hock makes a stronger, more efficient leg. Large formed hocks are better at absorbing concussion and generally make for a sounder joint. The hock should be:
> - Level with the top of the chestnut on the front leg: the chestnut resides a few inches above the knee.
> - Directly under the point of the buttocks, but slightly pointed inward when viewed from behind.
> - Wide from front to back and set on top of a sturdy cannon bone when viewed from the side.
>
> Cannon Bone: The hind cannon bone is usually longer and wider than the front cannon bone. From the side, you should be able to draw a line from the point of the buttock, down the back of the cannon to behind the heel.

Front Legs: Correct front legs will move in a straight line and promote the following:

- Good athletic ability
- Soundness
- Good stride
- Speed
- Agility

Abnormal or crooked front legs can lead to lameness by putting stress on the following:

- Bones
- Tendons
- Ligaments
- Muscle mass

From the front of the horse, you should be able to draw a straight line from the point of the shoulder down the center of the leg. This line should evenly split the forearm, knee, cannon, fetlock, pastern and hoof. From the side of the front leg, a straight line should be formed in front of the withers down the center of the front leg and touch at the heel. The cannon bone in the foreleg should be shorter than that of the rear leg.

Pasterns
The pastern angle to the toe should be forty to fifty five degrees. A nicely sloped hoof will transfer weight from the tendons to the upper leg. This decreases pressure on the tendons and maintains soundness. *(cited from: https://extension.umn.edu/horse-care-and-management/conformation-horse#pasterns-1159012)*

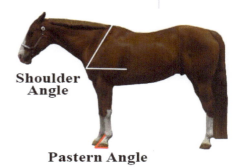

Conformation - Shoulders. 133

Locomotion - Gaits of the Horse

A basic understating of the gaits of a horse is important in analyzing form to function. A gait can be defined as a particular way of going, either natural or acquired. The essentials of a satisfactory way of going are straight-line action, long strides, briskness of gait and regularity of gait (meaning free, fluid and regular). Each gait is characterized by a distinctive rhythmic movement of the feet and legs. The natural gaits are walk, trot, pace, canter and gallop. Under domestication some gaits have been modified and are called acquired gaits. Some examples of these gaits are the running walk, rack and fox trot.

Gaits can also be classified according to how they ride. For instance hard gaited and easy gaited. Both of these are affected by conformation. For example, steep shouldered horses are usually hard gaited while long sloping shouldered horses are usually easy gaited.

Horse Walking [134]

Walk
- The walk is a four-beat gait; meaning each foot leaves and strikes the ground at different times.
- Speed averages from 3 ½ — 5 mph
- Natural gait for all breeds.
- Sequence of steps is unchanged in the ordinary, collected, or extended walk

Horse Trotting [134]

Trot
- The trot is a diagonal two beat gait
- Average speed 7-10 mph Extended 10-30 mph

- Believed to be a dominant genetic trait - it is a natural gait.
- Leg sequence unchanged at ordinary, collected or extended trot.
- Examples based on conformation (this will be explained in the next section)
    - Standardbred Horse - has a rapid, long ground-covering extended trot; used for harness racing; has a much longer period of suspension.
    - Hackney Horse - has a shorter stride; collected, animated trot; higher action and greater flexion of joints with little or no period of suspension.

Horse Cantering [134]

Canter
- The canter is a three-beat gait.
- Average speed 6-10 mph.
- Natural gait for all breeds.
- Base of support changes from one to two diagonal to one leg supporting weight.
- Sequence of steps changes depending on lead and direction of travel
- Leg sequence — right or left lead, depending which foreleg is leading; in a circular path, the inside foreleg and inside hind leg travel in a more advanced position.
    - Right lead: Left hind — 1st beat Right hind/left front — 2nd beat Right front — 3rd beat Period of suspension — after right front leaves ground
    - Left lead: Right hind — 1st beat Left hind/right front — 2nd beat Left front — 3rd beat Period of suspension — after left front leaves ground

Horse Galloping [134]

Gallop
- The gallop is a four-beat gait.
- Average speed of 12 -30 mph for most horses race horses at gallop 40 -44 mph - fastest gait of horse
- Natural gait to all breeds.
- Similar to canter but the paired diagonals do not land at the same time - extended to two beats: hind foot hits before the diagonal front foot. Has right or left lead depending on direction of travel. Period of suspension is after last front foot leaves ground.
- Sequence of steps will change depending on lead — race horses will change leads during race to shift weight and decrease fatigue on leading foreleg.
- Examples based on conformation (this will be explained in the next section)
    - horoughbred has been bred for his speed at this gait.

(cited from: https://animalrangeextension.montana.edu/equine/locomotion.html)

Other Gaits

Horses with extra movement patterns beyond the standard walk/trot/canter are called gaited horses. This trait can be inherited and is more common in some breeds than others. A horse's ability to perform these unique gaits is largely genetic. Certain breeds are more likely to have these special abilities, although many require further training to hone their skills. In 2012, Swedish researchers discovered that a single gene may control a horse's ability to pace – horses with the DMRT3 gene have the physical ability to pace, but those without it cannot. This was a significant discovery for Standardbreds, which are raced in harness as either trotters or pacers. Instead of spending years training a horse to race at these gaits at top speeds, breeders can figure out which horses are more likely to pace based on a DNA test. The genetic link also explains why some mustangs can gait and others cannot. Mustangs, with a lot of gaited bloodlines somewhere in their mystery pedigrees, sometimes keep the ability to gait and pass it down through generations without human intervention.

While some horses are taught to mimic specific movements, without a natural ability, they are not a truly gaited horse. Incredibly, this specific gene is linked back to one mutation in a horse's DNA thousands of years ago.

Running Walk (Tennessee Walking Horse): This is a four-beat gait that looks similar to a standard walk pattern, but is much faster. The back feet will significantly overstep the footfalls of the front feet in a movement called "overtracking" – the farther a horse overtracks, the smoother the walk will be.

Pace (Standardbred Horse): Like the trot, the pace is a two-beat gait. The horse's legs move together in lateral pairs: left hind and left foreleg, and vice versa.

Flying Pace (Icelandic Horse and Standardbred Horse): While the pace itself can be uncomfortable to ride, many Icelandic horses have a fast and smooth flying pace, which is what it sounds like – an exceptionally fast pace that rivals the speed of a gallop.

Rack/Tölt/Single-foot (American Saddlebred, and Icelandic Horse, Single-Footed Horse, Racking Horse): The rack (often called "single-foot") is a fast, lateral, four-beat gait that is synchronous— each foot meets the ground at equal, separate intervals. In Icelandic horses, the tölt is very similar to the rack and follows the same footfall pattern.

Fox-trot (Missouri Fox Trotter Horse): A four-beat gait, the fox-trot looks almost like a standard trot, but the front legs land just before the hind legs (in a true trot, they land at the same time).
(cited from: https://www.helpfulhorsehints.com/what-is-a-gaited-horse/)

Understanding Conformation and Locomotion

Kristi Wysocki, is a sporthorse breeding judge, FEI rider, trainer and rehab expert who worked as a professional engineer for 15 years before turning to horses professionally. She applied her engineering background to analyzing the form to function of horses. She stresses that conformation is largely dictated by the horse's bones. With a clear sense of the major skeletal systems, the next step is training the eye to see where the bones and connections are under the horse's coat. With the bones located, the next step is drawing straight lines between them to evaluate how the horse's parts will be able to work together. The eye for this can be developed by practicing with string on enlarged pictures of horses. In real life you can align straight sticks on a horse's body to determine angles and proportion. Encouraging results in any of these measurements are not a guarantee of proper carriage. Instead, they indicate that the horse will have an easier time doing its job and staying more sound while doing it. When a horse makes something look easy, it's usually because it is for them because they are built to do it.

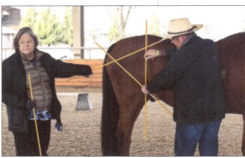

Kristi Wysocki shows where a horse's Center of Balance is on Lynn McEnespy's 6-year-old Hanoverian gelding, Wredford. [135]

The center of balance (or center of gravity) is one of several indicators that help predict the ability of the horse for a specific function. The horse's center of gravity is the balance point of his body. The center of balance occurs at the intersection of two lines: a diagonal line starting at the point of the scapula and a diagonal line running from the point of the buttock through the point of the hip. The engine of a horse is the hindquarters but, because of the heavy head and neck, the horse carries a greater amount of weight on its forehand. The horse can be trained to carry more of the cumbersome weight of the forehand with its haunches and thus the forehand lightens and makes the horse more agile and balanced. Therefore, if the horse is not well proportioned, this will be difficult to achieve.

Evaluating hindquarters in relation to desired function is also important. A triangle of lines connecting the point of hip, point of buttock and point of stifle can be used to evaluate the hindquarters. In a dressage horse, this is ideally an isosceles triangle in which the short side is the top line between the point of hip and point of buttock. In jumpers, it's typically better that all three sides be equal. A dressage horse needs to carry and lengthen and the jumper needs to carry and leap. In either type of horse, a good hindquarter triangle can make up for many other conformational weaknesses. *(cited from: https://practicalhorsemanmag.com/training/evaluating-horse-form-function-31701)*

From just these two examples it is easier to understand how the conformation of a horse can have an effect on the way of going and thus determine what function the horse is best suited.

Analyzing Conformation for Function

Today horses are used mostly for sport and pleasure. Some horses are still used for work purposes too. Understanding the conformation of the horse helps to determine if a horse is suited for a specific function. Following are a few uses of modern horses and an analysis of the ideal form for each of these uses. Breeds best fitting the form to function are also included in the analysis. But, this is IMPORTANT: Some horses defy the "rules". Even within types of conformation suited for a specific use, there are exceptions to the ideals. Some breeds are better suited for certain uses but, even within the breed there are subtle differences. This is why knowledge of consistently inherited traits within specific bloodlines of a breed is important!

Jumping

Hunters are judged subjectively on the degree to which they meet an ideal standard of manners, style, and way of going. Conversely, jumper classes are scored objectively, based entirely on a numerical score determined only by whether the horse attempts the obstacle, clears it and finishes the course in the allotted time. Jumper courses tend to be much more complex and technical than hunter courses because riders and horses are not being judged on style. *(cited from: https://en.wikipedia.org/wiki/Show_jumping)*

ANY breed of horse is suitable for jumping but there are some breeds that stand out; they are: Dutch Warmblood, Westphalian, Selle. [136]

1. Large, heavy horses are often slow off the ground and not as quick to respond as a lighter horse Very refined horses cannot always handle the scope (height and width the horse can jump) of top level jumps. A medium built horse is best for jumpers.
2. The best jumpers have longer backs which tend to be indicators of scope.
3. Jumpers should have clean, stout hocks, as these, along with the hindquarters, are the horse's engine. Hock angles for a jumper tend to be more closed. Again, this provides for more coiling and springing action.
4. A show jumper tends to have a long neck, set fairly high, to assist

with balance over the top of a fence. Their balance overall is usually level or slightly uphill.

5. The hindquarters provide the power, and the joint angles are critical in creating the upward trajectory. The point of hip to the point of buttock to the stifle should form an equilateral triangle. These are more closed angles than are seen in a dressage horse and permit a greater coiling and release of energy.

6. In a jumper, it is critical that the stifle be low and out of the way. The lower the stifle, the greater the scope and the longer his stride will be.

7. The critical conformation issue is, can the horse lift his knees high and out of the way? A successful jumper can have a shoulder that is either upright or laid back, but usually it is more the former than the latter. The scapula and humerus should be an open or steep angle (90° or greater) and the point of shoulder -- where the humerus and scapula meet is fairly high up toward the neck. A long shoulder with a more upright angle offers a greater range of motion, because the scapula can Rotate further backwards. This way it is easy for them to get their knees up.

8. The best jumpers usually have a long humerus. A long humerus generally means the horse will have a long stride and the ability to move the legs away from the rib cage, which helps make for a scopey jumper. In contrast, a more horizontal humerus or a shorter humerus will result in a shorter, choppier stride. A horizontally placed humerus also puts the leg farther under the horse, which makes it harder to get the front legs out of the way of the jump. *(cited from: https://www.behindthebitblog.com/2008/06/ dressage-versus-jumper-conformation.html)*

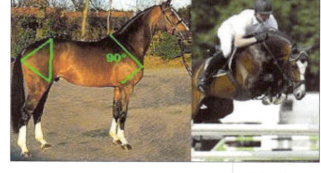

Balou du Rouet, show jumper stallion.[137]

Note the joint angles and how they fold up over a jump.[137]

145

Dressage

Dressage is a form of horse riding performed in exhibition and competition, as well as an art sometimes pursued solely for the sake of mastery. As an equestrian sport defined by the International Equestrian Federation, dressage is described as "the highest expression of horse training" where "horse and rider are expected to perform from memory a series of predetermined movements." *(cited from: https://en.wikipedia.org/wiki/Dressage)*

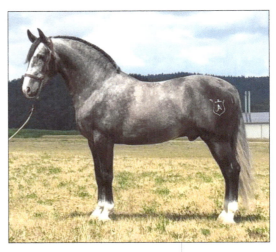

ANY breed of horse is suitable for dressage; after all dressage is a French word that means "training". Some breeds do excel though because of their conformation. The Spanish horses for instance are specifically bred for dressage and have been for centuries. [137a]

1. A dressage horse needs to have a lot of forward reach from the shoulder -- out rather than up. A laid back shoulder provides the freedom to extend the forelegs. It is also desirable in dressage because it places the wither farther back, and thus puts the rider further back, over the horse's center of gravity.
2. As with jumpers, dressage horses should have a long humerus. This increases the horse's ability to move the elbow away from the torso either toward the front or to the side, as in a half-pass.
3. In a dressage horse, a long forearm will help to make the uphill build that is so critical to dressage. Extra length in the forearm and shorter cannon bones are advantageous for height and soundness.
4. Both the jumper and the dressage horse will need a high neck set. The dressage horse tends to have a shorter, more upright neck than the jumper; the neck rises out of the withers at an angle that is close to 45 degrees. A long neck is not needed as a counterbalance (e.g., over the top of the fence), and it can actually make for a more difficult ride. While a longish neck is undeniably beautiful, it is not necessary and horses can use a long neck to evade the aids.
5. The hindquarters are similar to the jumping horse overall. A critical feature for both dressage and jumping horses is to have the

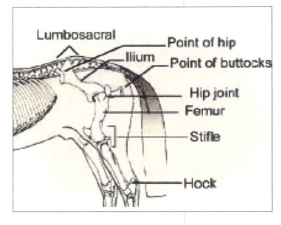

Dressage Hind End Conformation [138]

lumbosacral (LS) joint directly over the point of hip. This maximizes the power of the hind leg by making the most of the LS region's rotation. The LS is the only point of the vertebral column that allows significant amounts of flexion and extension.
6. Dressage horses tend to have a longer femur (point of buttock to stifle) and shorter, more level ilium (point of hip to point of buttocks) when compared to jumpers; their hip angles form a "7" where the downward stroke is the femur. They have a more open angle from ilium to femur, and while the stifle should be low, this is not as critical for the dressage horse.
7. Dressage horses will tend to have a straighter hock, as it will require less effort to close the joint angles and collect. *(cited from: https://www.behindthebitblog.com/2008/06/dressage-versus-jumper-conformation.html)*

Dressage Conformation
- "Uphill" or withers above point of hip.
- Length of body no more than 3X length of pelvis.
- Angles of pelvis and shoulders neither steep nor flat (do not confuse with sacral angle).
- Cervical curves equal and neither deep nor shallow, clear throat latch with room behind jaw to seat parotid gland.
- Deep loin coupling, avoid wry tail or clamped tail.
- Deep heart girth with well-sprung ribs (for lungs, heart, liver).
- Good bone, no crooked legs or tied in tendons, avoid splints.
- Smooth muscling, with NO lumps or excessively developed "underneck" or dip ahead of withers.

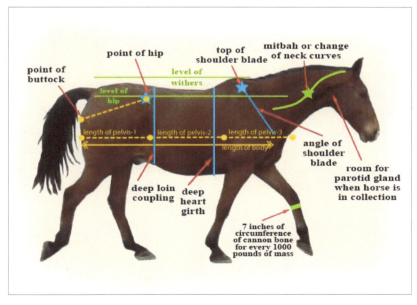

Overall Conformation for Dressage [139]

A Word About "Collection"

Collection is important for all horses, not just dressage horses. Collection is necessary to protect the horse's long term health. Many horses are always working on the forehand and this makes it difficult for them to do many things – from backing up softly to being able to turn easily to open and close gates. It's much more biomechanically beneficial for

Collection (top) raises the back and the forehand, so that the horse carries more weight on his hindquarters. Compared to a trot that is simply shortened, but not collected. (bottom) [140]

them, particularly when they are working, to be able to shift their balance to the hind end and have less weight on the forehand. When the horse is balanced on their hind end they will find it easier to carry out the movements that their handler or rider asks. When their weight isn't down on their shoulders and front legs it will be easier for them to step out to turn lightly and with softness. If they are doing

dressage exercises and they are in balance it will be easier for them. All of this will benefit their bodies physically and help to avoid work related strain. *(cited from: https://elaineheneyhorses.com/dressage-with-horses/)*

Even ancient horse trainers understood the importance of collection. Egyptian artwork of horses with chariots indicate that horse training centered on collection. Collection occurs when a horse's center of gravity is

shifted backwards. Energy is directed in a more horizontal trajectory with less forward movement. The long training necessary to achieve collection also rendered the horses both willing and obedient. Egyptian chariotry functioned in close order. Collection of the horse gave the drivers more control. Collection also enabled the driver to match twist and turn of the opposing infantry. *(cited from: Collection in Ancient Egyptian Chariot Horses, Kathy Hansen, Journal of the American Research Center in Egypt, Vol. 29 (1992), pp. 173-179 and https://en.wikipedia.org/wiki/Collection_%28horse%29*

Fragment of a limestone tomb-painting with a horse-drawn chariot above and cart drawn by onagars beneath. [141]

A Word About "Self Carriage"

Unlike the human shoulder girdle where the collarbones (clavicles) attach the arms to the body, a horse has none. Without a collarbone, a horse has no bony connection between its front limbs and trunk. Instead, strong muscles connect the inside of its shoulder blades to its rib cage, which act like slings and suspend the chest between the horse's two front limbs. Contraction of these sling muscles lift the trunk and withers between the shoulder blades, raising the withers to the same height or higher than the croup. When a horse travels without contraction of its sling muscles, the horse's motion looks downhill and on the forehand. The average horse carries 58 percent of its weight on its front legs and 42 percent on its hind legs. The horse must learn to move in an uphill balance by pushing upwards with its forelimbs. The hind legs can then function as they should by sitting to carry more weight and by providing pushing power. In essence, the heavy chest needs to be up and out of the way for the hind legs to push.

The sling muscles are extremely important to the self-carriage of the dressage horse. The goal in dressage training is to teach the horse to use its sling muscles throughout the workout. With time, these muscles get stronger and the persistent elevation allows the horse to push and hold its hind legs under the center of gravity through its motion to be even more pronounced and uphill.

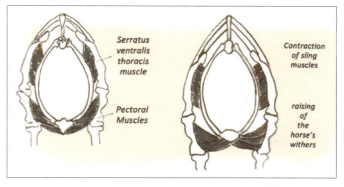

The Sling Muscles and Self-Carriage [142]

A horse's shoulders and trunk are heavy; therefore, in training and working toward collection with a horse, a rider must learn how to balance the chest and the trunk upwards so the hind legs can come underneath to provide propulsion and support. It's the balance of the trunk that allows the push from the hind legs to go through the horse's body without pushing it onto the forehand.

A horse's self-carriage is achieved through controlled tension of the muscle groups. There is a muscle ring that wraps around deep inside the horse through its back and abdominal muscles which allow it to maintain roundness of its back. The abdominal muscles encase the abdomen from the pelvis to the ribcage to the sternum. Contraction of these muscles and the back muscles allow the horse to be supple and loose to free its legs to push and carry all of its weight. *(cited from: https://www.swannequineosteo.com/blog/2017/12/5/equine-biomechanics-research-the-significance-of-a-horses-chest-sling-muscles)*

Racing

Differences between each racehorse can be very subtle since most thoroughbred horses are bred for running. Thus, it takes an experienced eye to notice the small details that could make huge impacts on the racecourse.

The definitive horse for racing is the Thoroughbred. Quarter Horses and Arabians are also used for racing but at venues for their specific breed; they do not compete against Thoroughbreds. Standardbreds are used for harness racing. [143]

1. The horse should be well balanced and in proportion. If the frame of the horse is too light to carry its muscle weight, it could lead to severe injuries.
2. The feet withstand the pressure of the horse running. Consider proportion, substance and size of the hoof. The underside of the hoof should have a round, slightly oval shape with some depth. Some believe that larger feet indicate an aptitude for turf. Look for balanced feet on both sides and symmetry. Avoid misshapen, dished or cracked feet.
3. The pastern should be at a 45-degree angle. Its length should be proportionate - too long a pastern could indicate weakness and tendon strain, while if too short it may absorb too much concussion thus stressing the bone structure.
4. As with the pastern, the ankle joint size should be proportionate to the rest of the leg.
5. Ideally, the cannon bone should be short, strong and have mass. From the front, the cannon bones should appear straight and of the same length.
6. Bones in and leading to the knee should line up in a balanced manner - not tilting forward ("over at the knee") or back ("back at the knee"). It is best if the knees are set squarely on the top of the cannon bones, not off to one side or another - "offset knees."
7. The shoulder should have the same slope or angle as the pastern. Stride length is largely determined by the shoulder.
8. The neck should be sufficient in scope so as to provide adequate wind for the horse and be well tied in at the withers, while not being too low or "ewe necked".
9. The chest should be broad and appear powerful. Narrow chests or slab-sided horses are said to lack power
10. The head should be broad enough to permit adequate air passage. Generally, the distance from the back of the jaw to where the head ties into the neck should be about the size of a fist.

11. The distance from the withers to top of croup or hips should match the length of the horse's neck from the poll to the withers.
12. The croup or hip should have a gentle slope - not too steep or flat. The gaskin should depict strength.
13. A horse's hocks should not be straight as a post nor curved so deeply as to be sickle hocked or behind the body like a German Shepherd Dog. The horse should be standing balanced and straight.
14. The horse should move straight toward and away from you. The horse should not toe-in or toe-out as it walks. The horse should overstep, (do the hind feet reach beyond the front hoof prints?)
15. The horse's head should not bob unusually when walking as this may indicate soreness or lameness. Walk - Look for a smooth long stride. *(cited from: https://www.horseracing.com/blog/conformation-of-a-racehorse/ and http://www.favourstud.com/images/Conformation.pdf)*

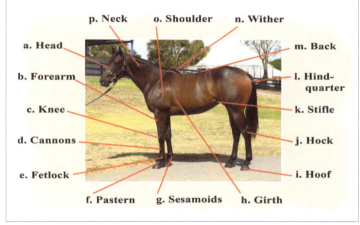

Race Horse Conformation [144]

a. *Head: Expressive, intelligent eye. Broad jowls which provides ample room for the windpipe. Big, broad nostrils.*
b. *Forearm: Straight, good bone and strong muscle tone. The forearm will be larger in sprinters than stayers.*
c. *Knee: Symmetrical, ideally flat, smooth and tight to touch, forward facing.*
d. *Cannons: Proportionally shorter in sprinters, hard, straight and flat. Tendon connecting the knee and fetlock should be hard and straight.*
e. *Fetlock: Strong, tight, round, symmetrical.*
f. *Pastern: At 45 degree angle to the cannon bone and on the same angle as the hoof and shoulder.*
g. *Sesamoids: Two bones on rear of fetlock joint. should be tight and not prominent.*
h. *Girth: The more depth the better-more room for the cavity containing the lungs and heart.*
i. *hoof: neat, medium sized, smooth and without ridges. Two front and two hind should be matching pairs.*
j. *Hock: Large joint midway on the rear leg. Strong transit joint that should be clean and efficient.*
k. *Stifle: Front side of the thigh at the top of the rear legs. Strong and flexible area of muscle and tendon.*
l. *Hindquarter: The powerhouse of the horse. Strong, powerful, deep and well angled. Look for good muscle tone of the gaskin (stifle to hock).*
m. *Back: Strong and short. Back should be strongly muscled with the loins short and firm.*
n. *Wither: Arched and highest point of horses back. Should not be too prominent nor too flat.*
o. *Shoulder: Sprinters tend to have straighter and more heavily muscled shoulders that stayers.*
p. *Neck: Strong and in proportion to the body, set evenly on the shoulders.*

151

Harness Racing

Some harness racing horses are trotters and others are pacers; it is very important that they are able to perform their specific gaits. Standardbeds are the definitive harness racing horse. Due to the influence of the Morgan, the Standardbred's conformation is quite different from the Thoroughbred's. The Standardbred is much hardier in appearance.

American Standardbred 144a

1. Haunches: Bred for speed, the Standardbred has high haunches - usually 1" higher than the withers.
2. Backs: Their backs are longer than a Thoroughbred and they should also have a long underline
3. Size: The average height for the Standardbred is between 14.2hh and 16hh; their weight is usually between 900 to 1,200 lbs.
4. Front end: Standrabreds have broad chests and an extremely powerful, sloping shoulder. A successful harness racer should have a shoulder angle and angle of pastern of 75° - although you will find horses with a lesser angle.
5. Legs: They should have good strong, straight legs, strong tendons and hard feet. Legs are shorter and stronger than a Thoroughbred's. The pacing Standardbred, especially one that has race trained or raced, has a slightly turned out conformation in the hind foot (toe-out) that aids the pacing gate. This may also be evident in a trotting Standardbred.
6. Head: The head is less defined than that of the Thoroughbred and has more substance with a wide brow.

(cited from: https://www.horseracing.com/blog/buying-and-owning-a-standardbred/ and https://www.thehorseguide.com/horse-breed-information/warmblood-breeds/standardbred/ and https://allaboutstandardbreds.blogspot.com/2009/07/standardbred-breeding-whats-in.html and http://www.spphav.org.au/index.php?page=the-standardbred)

The Standardbred horse is considered to be the fastest harness horse in the world. Harness racing has been a passion in the United States since the early 1800s. Then, the Morgan horse reigned as the supreme harness horse. But, an event occurring in 1849 that ended the Morgan Dynasty. This event was the foaling of a horse named Hambletonian 10, the foundation sire of the Standardbred horse. The breed gains its name from the fact that a horse must meet a certain "standard" of either timed speed at the mile or breeding in order to be properly registered. The increased brilliance of the Standardbred breed itself has reduced times for the mile by a minute – down 30 percent from original record.

Trotter [145]

Pacer [146]

153

Endurance

Endurance riding is based on controlled long-distance races. Most endurance rides are either 50 or 100 miles The winning horse is the first one to cross the finish line while stopping periodically to pass a veterinary check that deems the animal in good health and fit to continue. *(cited from: https://en.wikipedia.org/wiki/Endurance_riding)*

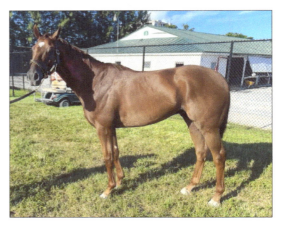

Seaman - a long distance runner. Photo: David Racing LLC. [147]

1. Balance. All of the horse's body parts should flow together. His weight should be evenly distributed from front to back and top to bottom. The hindquarters should not be disproportionately larger than the shoulders or vice versa. Nor should the front end be higher or lower than the hind end. The bone thickness should be consistent throughout the horse, as well. A thick-bodied horse supported by toothpick legs is going to get in trouble. There are 3 major angles – shoulder, hip, and pastern. All should be about equal and compared to 45 degrees. (picture 1) Ideally the horse should be box shaped, with a butt that isn't higher then the wither. There are 4 measurements that should be approximately he same length (neck, shoulder, back, hip - blue lines in picture 2). The green line in picture 2 represents the underline. The underline should be longer then the topline (represented as the dotted blue line, which is also the length of the back).
2. Straightness. The legs are basically weight-bearing columns, which are strongest when they're straight. Any extreme deviation from straightness causes torque in the joints and soft tissues, which can lead to lameness over time. A horse who is over at the knee (the knee is in front of the alignment of the rest of the leg when observed from the side) is generally preferable to a horse who is calf-kneed (the knee is behind the alignment of the rest of the leg). The former is more of a blemish, whereas the latter is a weakness. A mild degree of cow hocks (the hocks are closer together than the rest of the hind legs when viewed from behind) also may not necessarily be a problem. But it is best to avoid any severe deviation from normal.
3. The sloping shoulder angle that riders idealize in other sports doesn't seem to mean much in endurance.
4. Good feet are critical in endurance, not only because of the many miles covered but because the footing is often rocky, hard and otherwise unpredictable. Look for concave soles, thick walls and heels that aren't extremely high or low.
5. Aesthetics are not important. A horse with an ugly head may be just as competitive as a prettier horse, so long as he breathes well through his nostrils and sees well in both daylight and dark (longer endurance races start and/or end in the dark). Ewe necks, long

backs and "hunter's bump" are rarely problematic. Short backs, on the other hand, can cause saddle rubs, simply because the back edge of the saddle ends up so close to the croup.

6. Smaller, lighter-framed horses tend to excel in endurance, perhaps because of their higher-surface-area-to-body-mass ratio, which helps their body temperatures cool faster. The best endurance mounts stand about 15 hands. Those who excel in steep mountain races tend to have sturdy bodies with bulkier, more powerful muscles, whereas those winning the flatter, faster races tend to be lighter with leaner, more streamlined muscles.

7. Movement. Watching a potential endurance horse in motion is critical. All of the above qualities can be evaluated in a horse standing still, but they won't tell you what you most need to know: how efficiently and sustainably he travels down a trail. He must move fluidly and effortlessly, carrying himself in a natural, neutral balance. He should also possess a great deal of scope - the ability to lengthen and shorten his stride easily - which will help him cover more ground more efficiently. Any dramatic deviation in the gaits, such as paddling or winging, not only wastes energy but also can lead to injury. Even excessive suspension in the gaits a quality much sought after in other disciplines can be a drawback, as it wastes too much energy pushing the horse up into the air rather than down the trail.

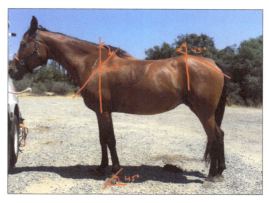

Picture 1 - 3 major angles – shoulder, hip, and pastern. All should be about equal and compared to 45 degrees. [148]

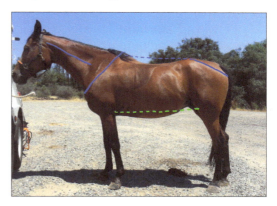

Picture 2 - Angles and proportions of neck, shoulder, back and hip. These 4 "lines" should be approximately the same in length. The green line represents the underline. The underline should be longer then the topline (represented as the dotted blue line, which is also the length of the back). [148a]

All of these recommendations address the ideal physical qualities of a good endurance horse. However, there are many essential qualities that are harder to measure: stamina, heart, toughness and an uncanny sense of where to place his feet on the trail without tripping on rocks or roots. These qualities have been bred into Arabians for centuries, hence their great competitive success. But you can find them in horses of almost any breed. *(cited from: https://practicalhorsemanmag.com/health-archive/whats-the-ideal-endurance-horse-conformation and https://melnewton.com/2015/the-way-i-see-it/)*

Saddle Seat

Saddle Seat is one of the less commonly seen styles of riding today and it is not really used for anything outside the show ring. This style of riding is known for being very flashy and active. Some of the horse breeds used for Saddle Seat today were originally used as plantation horses due to their comfort and speed at the trot which is the gait that can be maintained for distances.

American Saddlebred 148

1. *Head*–well-shaped with large, wide-set expressive eyes, gracefully shaped ears set close together on top of the head and carried alertly; a straight face line with a relatively fine muzzle and large nostrils and a clean and smooth jaw line.
2. *Neck*–long, arched and well-flexed at the poll with a fine, clean throatlatch.
3. *Withers*–well defined and prominent.
4. *Shoulders*–deep and sloping.
5. *Back*–strong and level with well sprung ribs.
6. *Croup*–level with a well carried tail coming out high.
7. *Legs*–The front leg should set well forward under the shoulder. The line of the hind leg, in a natural stance, should be vertical from the point of the buttock to the back edge of the cannon bone. The forearms and hindquarters are well muscled to the knees and hocks. Legs are straight with broad flat bones, sharply defined tendons and sloping pasterns.
8. *Hooves*–good and sound, open at the heel, neither toed in or toed out.*(cited from: https://equinehusbandry.ces.ncsu.edu/wp-content/uploads/2015/02/Conformation-of-the-American-Saddlebred.pdf?fwd=no)*

Breeds commonly used for Saddle Seat include: American Saddlebred, Morgan, Arab, Tennessee Walker and Friesian.

General Appearance

Type: Symmetry, overall ease of identification as an American Saddle bred

Quality: Bone clean, dense, fine, yet indicating substance. Tendons and joints sharply defined, hide and hair fine, general refinement

Temperament: Gentle disposition, active, intelligent

Conformation for Saddle Seat [149]

1. *Head* (carried relatively high; size and dimensions in proportion, clear-cut features, well-chiseled, smooth jaw line)
2. *Muzzle* (fine; nostrils large; lips thin, trim, even)
3. *Eyes* (wide-set, large, full, bright, clear, expressive, lid thin)
4. *Ears* (small, fine, alert, out of top of head, pointed, set close)
5. *Neck* (long, supple, well-crested; throatlatch clean; head well set on)
6. *Shoulders* (long, sloping, deep, muscular)
7. *Forearms* (long, broad, muscular)
8. *Knees* (straight, wide, deep, strongly supported)
9. *Cannons* (short, broad, flat, tendons sharply defined, set well back)
10. *Pasterns* (long, sloping, 45-degree angle with vertical, smooth, strong)
11. *Hooves* (round, uniform, straight; frog large and elastic; heels wide)
12. *Legs* (sinewy -- when viewed from front, a vertical line from the point of the shoulder should divide the leg and foot into two lateral halves; viewed from the side, the same line should pass through the center of the elbow joint and the center of the foot)
13. *Withers* (well-defined, well-finished at top, extending well into the back)
14. *Chest* (medium-wide, deep)
15. *Ribs* (well-sprung, long, close)
16. *Back* (short, level, strong, broad)
17. *Flanks* (deep, long, full flank, not tucked, low underline)
18. *Hips* (broad, round, smooth)
19. *Croup* (long, level, smooth; no goose rump)
20. *Tail* (comes out high from back; well-carried)
21. *Thighs* (full, muscular)
22. *Gaskins* (broad, muscular)
23. *Hocks* (straight, wide, point prominent, deep, clean-cut, smooth, well-supported)
24. *Cannons* (short, broad, flat, tendons sharply defined)
25. *Pasterns* (long, sloping, smooth, strong)
26. *Hooves* (slightly less round than in front, uniform, straight, sole concave; frog large and elastic; heels wide and full)
27. *Legs* (viewed from the rear, a vertical line dropped from the point of the buttock should divide the leg and foot into lateral halves; viewed from the side, the same vertical line from the point of the buttock should touch the hind edge of the cannon from the hock to the fetlock)

157

Western Performance

Many people choose to enjoy their western type horses in competitive events. These activities can be either individual or team events. Some are judged by a set of written rules and specifications and other competitive activities are timed events. These events include: barrel racing, reining, cutting, roping, working cow horse and team penning. The conformation preferred for these events is described as follows:

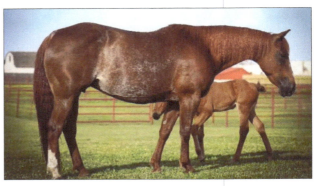

Conformation for Western Performance 150

1. Head: small muzzle, big eye, straight face, short mouth (feels better in hands), clean throat latch
2. Neck: top line of neck should be level with hip
3. Withers: prominent (will hold saddle well)
4. Hip: need good length of hip and low tail set
5. Chest: neck should come high out of chest, not low, avoid a wide chest (makes horse heavy on front)
6. Flank: should be deep from croup to belly (makes it easy to have a strong stop which cutting and reining horses need)
7. Gaskins: need to be strong and have good muscle on the inside (necessary for stopping)
8. Hock: avoid too much angle, need moderate ankle for stopping, need to be under hind end, not behind
9. Cannon bone: should be shorter than upper leg (prevents excessive motion which wastes energy)
10. Hind end: should be larger than front end so that horse is light in front and strong behind
11. Fetlock: avoid long fetlock (weak) avoid short fetlock (rough to ride)
12. Hind legs: cutting horse needs to be able to spread hind legs, reining horses needs to be able to slide so no need to spread hind legs *(cited from: Larry Trocha performance horse analysis https://www.youtube.com/watch?v=N8cSY-SHBpA)*

Breeds commonly used for Western performance are Quarter Horse, Mustang, Paint, Appaloosa and Morgan.

Barrel Racing [151]

Roping [152]

Reining [153]

Cutting [154]

159

Trail/Packing

"Pretty" does not matter with a trail horse! When you are out there on the trails navigating timber, mud, and streams, it quickly becomes clear that beauty truly is in the eye of the beholder. The smoothness and safety of the ride is due to several factors: bone, pasterns, foot quality, back length, the horse's natural gait, shoulder slope, size relative to the hindquarter. Conformation characteristics of a trail/packing horse include:

Arabians, Morgans, Tennessee Walkers, Rocky Mountain Horse, Appaloosa, Draft crosses and Mules are breeds often used for trail and packing. [155]

1. Bone: From an outfitter's and trail rider's perspective, bigger bone is generally a good thing. Riding over rough, rocky, muddy ground with heavy loads can be a punishing activity. Bigger bone means bigger joints and tendons. Joint problems are often the result of tendon issues.
2. Pasterns: You will generally notice less stumbling with a stout pastern. Although the highly sloped, longer pastern may mean smoother riding and more comfort in the arena, this quality is not as durable on the trail as a stout pastern with less slope.
3. Foot: Avoid thin soles and "shelly" hooves.
4. Backs: Long backed horses don't navigate tough terrain as well as shorter backed horses, similar to the way a four-wheel-drive vehicle with a very long wheelbase navigates compared to a four-wheel-drive vehicle with a shorter wheelbase. A flat-backed, low-withered horse exaggerates motion. Many riders have slid, skid, and bounced to the ground because the saddle slipped on a flat-backed horse.

Appaloosa Horse [156]

160

5. Withers: High withered horses are not desirable. Often high withers means that extra effort is needed to find a saddle with a high gullet and thicker padding and cutouts must be used in the wither area. Conversely, a horse with little or no withers can be a real problem because there is not enough wither there to secure the saddle or the load.

Pack Horse and Mule with Rifle/Bow Scabbard [157]

6. Muscle: Several breeds of horses have leaner muscle which is well suited to long days on the trail. Longevity and muscle power are needed to push up steep slopes, through mud, up banks and to stabilize loads in swift water. Therefore, some muscle is good, particularly in the upper leg areas of the gaskin and stifle.

7. Neck: A long neck and fine throatlatch are not necessary; Turning left, right and back originates from a soft mind rather than from a fine throatlatch.

Draft-Cross Horse [158]

8. Chest: A medium or wider chest is preferred both for better wind and because a wider base is better in rough going. However, an overly wide chest on a base narrow horse, with feet coming close together on the ground, is a fault to watch out for.

9. Legs: Knees that back under the forelimb is a fault in a trail horse. Slightly toed-in or toed-out conformation is not a serious fault, but if the horse swings its feet out noticeably or is very pigeon toed, its stability under trail conditions is compromised. Cow hocked is another common fault, but many cold blooded draft horses are cow hocked and are sure footed on the trail.

10. Size: Remember - you may need to get on and off so make sure you can do that without a mounting block nearby. *(cited from: https://www.horsejournals.com/riding-training/more-disciplines/trail/trail-tips-conformationtrail-horse and https://www.horsejournals.com/trimming-shoeing/good-hoof-bad-hoof)*

161

Work Horses

Whether they are clearing forests, plowing fields or transporting people and things, throughout world history we've long relied on horses for the strength and power we lack for certain tasks. Needs and conformation characteristics of a work horse are listed below.

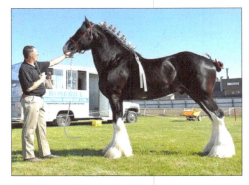

Clydesdale [159]

1. Horses can typically pull about 1/10 of their body weight in "dead weight," such as a plow or fallen log. If you add wheels to the load (e.g. put a log on a cart), an average horse can then pull 1.5 times its body weight over a longer distance. For shorter distances, this number may go up considerably—six times the horse's body weight, or even more, depending on the breed.
2. Physically fit horses with broader shoulders and big strong legs can pull more than finely-boned or out of shape horses.

Belgian [160]

3. Pairing horses increases load capability, or how much weight they can pull together.
4. Draft horses are bred for heavier tasks like plowing fields and pulling heavy loads. Draft breeds may be referred to as "cold blooded." This term simply references their temperament—calm, quiet and gentle giants.
5. When it comes to pulling heavy loads, draft breeds truly excel. A typical draft horse weighs 1,600 lbs or more. This is quite a bit larger than the average riding horse, which weighs in around 1,000 lbs.

Percheron [161]

6. Draft horses are bred to pull; they tend to have an uphill build with short, strong, high-set necks and powerful shoulders.

7. Draft horses are naturally large averaging between 15 to 18 HH and incredibly muscular in their conformation.
8. The head is large and broad with a large and kind eye. The nose varies between breeds with some drafts like the Shire having a Roman nose.
9. The neck is thick set with a naturally muscular crest with many drafts having low withers and a short back, with upright powerful shoulders which when combined with their round hindquarters allows them to easily pull very large loads.
10. Depending on the breed, the lower limbs may have extensive feathering such as is seen with Clydesdale or may be clean limbed as with the Suffolk Punch. Draft breeds usually have very thick mane and tails and great depth to their girth area.

Suffolk Punch [165]

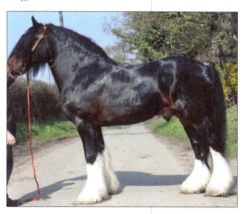

Shire [166]

(cited from: https://horserookie.com/how-much-weight-can-a-horse-pull/ and https://thehorse.com/194403/built-to-last-ideal-equine-conformation/ and https://www.equestrianandhorse.com/draft/breeds.html)

Popular draft breeds include the Clydesdale, Belgian, Percheron, Suffolk Punch and Shire.

163

A Horse is a Horse

To the untrained eye, a horse is a horse. But, after learning a little about form to function, the differences in conformation are very noticeable.

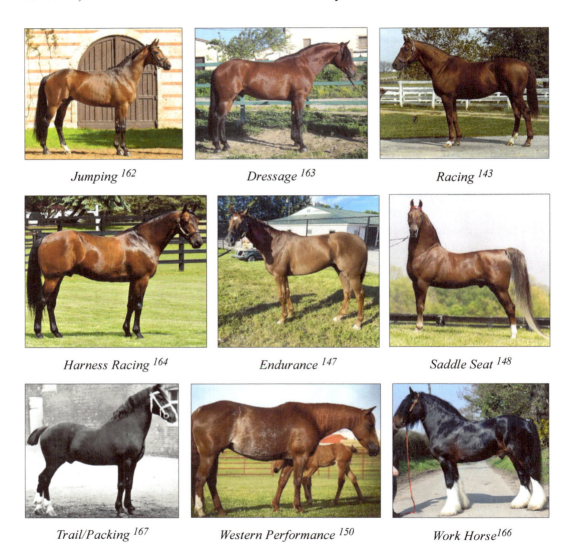

Jumping [162]   Dressage [163]   Racing [143]

Harness Racing [164]   Endurance [147]   Saddle Seat [148]

Trail/Packing [167]   Western Performance [150]   Work Horse [166]

Other Considerations

It's not just conformation that determines if a horse is suited for a specific function. Temperament is an important issue that must be taken into consideration; it affects their mental and psychological responses. There is no "good" or "bad" temperament, but a type of temperament adapted to a given usage can be defined. Indeed, according to their temperament, certain horses will be more apt at learning certain

168

tasks, better adapted to certain riders. The best temperament for a horse depends on what it is to be used for and the personal preference of the owner or rider. A nervous or novice rider will need a calm and predictable horse. Riders who want to compete at a higher level will normally opt for a horse with a temperament with a bit of fizz and boldness; these are horses which are intelligent and hard-working and will respond well to pressure in a competition situation.

Tracing bloodlines and evaluating siblings is one way to determine temperament but, just like human children, each horse is an individual. For some, looking at whorls (cowlicks) is a time honored method of judging a horse's temperament. Linda Tellington-Jones, of T-Touch fame, says you can analyze the shape of your horse's head, eyes, ears, chin, jowl and profile to learn their innate personality. Linda Parelli has coined the term Horsenality and how she defines temperament with four main characteristics: Left-Brained (Dominant); Right-Brained (Unconfident); Introvert (More Whoa); and Extrovert (More Go). She has developed a valuable assessment tool with a Horsenality Chart in the Parelli book, "HorseManShip". For more than 2,000 years, traditional Chinese medicine (TCM) has evaluated temperament according to the 5 Elements; Fire, Wood, Earth, Metal, Water. In her book, "Horse Harmony," Madalyn Ward, DVM, uses this model to define different horse personalities as well as the best training, occupation, diet and management approach for each type. *(cited from: https://www.pathintl.org/63-resources/resources-landing-page/1441-equine-tips-evaluating-horse-temperament-personality)*

In recent years, much research has gone into establishing a consistent and reliable horse temperament measurement. A horse temperament scale is an assessment of the temperament of an individual horse or horse breed. This assessment is then used to determine where the horse sits on a temperament scale, enabling us to compare it against other horses. A horse temperament scale will normally range from 1 – the calmest type of horse to 10, which would be the most excitable type of horse. Researchers have tried to create temperament analysis tools that give consistent and repeatable results. However, they have found that some people struggle to objectively analyze a horse's temperament, favoring certain breeds or types over others. *(cited from: https://www.besthorserider.com/horse-temperament-scale/)*

Scientists make a distinction between temperament and personality. Temperament is the innate character of each individual. This will be modified by the environment, particularly by the mother and living conditions (social life, different experiences with man, breaking-in conditions, and usage….) This gives rise to the personality of the animal. This term, although slightly "anthropomorphic", is the term used in current international scientific literature. Within the framework of a collaboration between INRA and the French National Stud/IFCE, Léa Lansade conducted a longitudinal study over a period of three years with the aim of defining a temperament model in the horse. The dimensions were each defined by a scientific approach showing their stability in time and with regard to similar situations. This work followed other studies conducted by other French or foreign authors, more specifically those conducted by the Rennes University. The model is composed of five large dimensions:

- Emotivity: the tendency to react more or less strongly to sudden events (e.g: surprise) or new events (e.g: walking over an alien surface)
- Herd instinct: can the horse bear to be separated from the other horses?
- Locomotive activity: Does horse move spontaneously or not at all?
- Reactivity to humans: Does the horse go easily towards an unfamiliar human being?
- Sensorial sensitivity: Does the horse react more or less strongly to stimuli, specifically touch?

These dimensions can be predicted as early as 8 months old, and appear stable up to the age of three. They are measurable and for each dimension one or several tests have been defined so as to place the horse's reactions on a scale of marks: temperament tests have thus been developed. *(cited from: https://equipedia.ifce.fr/fileadmin/bibliotheque/7.Technical_information/The-horse-s-temperament.pdf)*

There are even some "decoders" that try to match horse temperament with owner personality. When it comes right down to to it though, ask ten horse owners about evaluating temperament and you'll get ten different answers on how to determine a horse's temperament.

Few scientific papers on this issue have been published on the topic of horse temperament however, in 2021 a study was done to determine the relationship of horse temperament with breed, age, sex, and body characteristics; it was a questionnaire-based study. A web-based survey consisting of a 32-item questionnaire was used to clarify the associations of sex, breed, age and body characteristics with a horse's temperament. The owners of a total of 112 horses from different countries (Egypt, Jordan, Palestine, and Iraq) were recruited to fill in the questionnaire about their horses. Analysis of the data revealed that the questionnaire was reliable. The results showed statistically significant associations of sex and breed with temperament with 89.7% and 108.3%, while there was no significant association between age and temperament. The results also clarified significant associations between body characteristics (color, head and body marks, leg marks, and whorls) and temperament.

The study showed there was a relationship between sex and temperament; more respondents defined geldings as calm, reliable, trainable, and predictable; and mares as safe, bossy, trainable, willing, and as having a good attitude; while some respondents labeled stallions as being difficult, while a large proportion of them labeled stallions as being bossy, trainable and having a good attitude.

167

A horse's breed was found to have a direct association with its temperament; breed can affect a horse's reactions toward humans. It is therefore predicted that horse breeds differ in their personalities.

Regarding the relationship between age and temperament, the study revealed that 2-year-old horses were less manageable than younger ones.

A horse's coat color has long been considered to reflect its temperament. The results in this study suggest that silver horses are more cautious in novel situations, rather than more reactive in fearful situations. They also revealed the relatively common opinion that different coat colors are related to personality traits such as calmness, boldness, or nervousness. Previous studies reported that black mares were more independent than bay mares. This to some extent agrees with the survey results that suggested a relationship between a horse's coat color and its temperament. It is believed that the relationship between coat color and temperament is associated with the shared signaling pathways utilized by neurons and melanocytes, resulting in pleiotropic traits of coat color and behavior in many mammalian species.

Colors and Markings [169]

Hair whorls in horses are considered a constant form of identification for horses, since a whorl does not change in direction or location during a horse's lifetime. Whorls can thus be considered the equine tantamount of fingerprints in humans. Horses with two whorls, either side by side or one above the other, tend to be more reactive than average. They also tend to become disturbed for no apparent reason and at unexpected moments. The findings also agree with a previous study that noted that horses with double whorls on the face tend to be overly reactive or highly strung to novel stimuli. The relationship between temperament and this body characteristic has also been explained by research showing that skin and brain tissue come from the same layer of cells (ectoderm) during embryonic development. As embryonic cells migrate to form the fetus, skin and brain cells are closely intertwined, particularly at the scalp, explaining how this hair formation could be related to personality. It was also added that, although hair whorls cannot completely predict a horse's temperament or performance, they might be worth taking into consideration when purchasing horses.

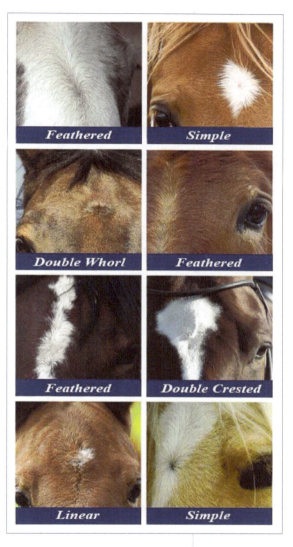

Horse Whorls 170

This questionnaire-based study proved that purchasers can predict a horse's temperament from its sex, breed, and body characteristics, including coat color, body and leg marks, and whorls. *(cited from: https://bjbas.springeropen.com/articles/10.1186/s43088-021-00133-8)*

Temperament is an important issue that should be taken into consideration when purchasing horses.

169

Conclusion

It's hard for us, today, to imagine being dependent on a horse but remember, horses have been around longer than cars and planes. Horses have played an important role in the history of the world. Whether ridden or driven, horses were the means by which cultures intermingled, people were able to share communications, wars were waged and nations developed. For many people, looking out the window at a horse in a pasture is a serene reminder of human history yet still, the horse brings with it all the potential of more adventures and opportunities to come.

Tyson and Hark, in a snowy paddock. Photo by Mary Chris Foxworthy [171]

Sources and Further Reading

Evolution of the horse
https://socratic.org/questions/what-is-the-correct-sequence-of-horse-evolution

Eohippus
https://paleontologyworld.com/exploring-prehistoric-life/evolution-horse
https://www.britannica.com/animal/perissodactyl
https://www.thoughtco.com/eohippus-dawn-horse-1093222

Mesohippus, Miohippus
https://en.wikipedia.org/wiki/Mesohippus
https://www.thoughtco.com/miohippus-miocene-horse-1093245
https://fossil.fandom.com/wiki/Miohippus

Epihippus, Orohippos,
http://www.prehistoric-wildlife.com/species/e/epihippus.html
https://www.britannica.com/animal/horse/Evolution-of-the-horse#ref239136
https://www.floridamuseum.ufl.edu/fossil-horses/gallery/orohippus/

Parahippus, Merychippis, Pliohippus
https://en.wikipedia.org/wiki/Parahippus
https://www.thoughtco.com/merychippus-ruminant-horse-1093241
https://www.britannica.com/animal/Merychippus
https://www.equineguelph.ca/equimania/DomesticationTimeline
https://www.equineguelph.ca/equimania/DomesticationTimeline/pliohippus.html

Dinohippus
https://equineguelph.ca/learn_objects/evolutiontimeline/dinohippus.html

Equus
http://netnebraska.org/basic-page/television/wild-horses-evolution
https://www.equineguelph.ca/equimania/DomesticationTimeline/equus.html

Equine family today
https://www.britannica.com/topic/list-of-horses-zebras-and-asses-2058537

Chapter 2
http://horse-stall.net/horse-articles/history-of-horse-breeding.htm
https://thehorse.com/152562/history-of-the-horse/
https://en.wikipedia.org/wiki/Rope
https://agapepetservices.com/make-horse-human-relationships-unique/

171

https://aaep.org/sites/default/files/issues/proceedings-08proceedings-z9100108000001.PDF
https://horses.extension.org/relating-form-to-function-horses-frontlegs-front-view/
https://agecroft.wordpress.com/ancient-breeds-of-horse/ evolution of types
http://www.levlab.ucsd.edu/publications/nahaltillah/
https://www.academia.edu/8814160/The_presence_of_horse_in_ancient_Egypt_and_the_problem_of_veracity_of_the_horseshoe_magic_in_the_ancient_Egyptian_folklore_and_mythology_pp_321_340
https://en.wikipedia.org/wiki/Horses_in_warfare *refer to for tack and type of horse
https://www.archaeology.org/issues/180-1507/features/3349-warhorses
https://www.bionity.com/en/encyclopedia/Horses_in_warfare.html
http://www.fao.org/livestock-systems/global-distributions/horses/en/
https://www.history.com/topics/ancient-middle-east/sumer
http://teachinghistory100.org/objects/about_the_object/ur_standard
https://spiritedhorse.wordpress.com/2017/12/23/the-standard-of-ur/
https://www.texasgateway.org/resource/natural-selection-and-selective-breeding
https://www.artbycrane.com/horse_breeds/light_horse_breeds/wild_horses.html
http://stablemade.com/horsecare/horsebreeds/kertag.htm breed types-Mongolian
https://www.archaeology.wiki/blog/2019/09/04/two-unplundered-tombs-discovered-at-aidonia-cemetery/
https://stasaart.wordpress.com/2017/02/09/horse-in-ancient-greece/ ancient Greece pix
https://ezinearticles.com/?Greece-Horses-in-Ancient-Greece&id=971992
https://equusmagazine.com/blog-equus/coats-many-colors-dna-ancient-horses-54695 colors
https://www.karwansaraypublishers.com/awblog/chariots-and-horses-in-the-homeric-world/
Homeric, British and Cyrenaic Chariots, J. K. Anderson, American Journal of Archaeology, Vol. 69, No. 4 (Oct., 1965), pp. 349-352
Collection in Ancient Egyptian Chariot Horses, Kathy Hansen, Journal of the American Research Center in Egypt, Vol. 29 (1992), pp. 173-179
https://en.wikipedia.org/wiki/Collection_%28horse%29
https://www.touregypt.net/featurestories/chariots.htm
https://trustedbyzantinemedievalcoins.wordpress.com/2021/04/04/horses-on-ancient-greek-roman-coins-including-races-chariots-pegasus-45/
Horse Care as Depicted on Greek Vases before 400 B.C., Mary B. Moore, Metropolitan Museum Journal, Vol. 39 (2004), pp. 8, 35-67
file:///C:/Users/Mary%20Chris/Downloads/Xenophon-Horseman-

ship_2015Edit.pdf
https://itchyfish.com/the-thessalian-rare-horse-breed-of-antiquity/
https://historandmor.blogspot.com/2016/08/the-thessalian-cavalry.html
file:///C:/Users/Mary%20Chris/Downloads/Horse_and_Horsemen_on_Classical_and_Hell.pdf
https://www.nationalgeographic.org/media/kingdoms-kush/
The Horses of Kush, Lisa A. Heidorn, Journal of Near Eastern Studies, Vol. 56, No. 2 (Apr., 1997), pp. 105-11
Foreign Chariotry and Cavalry in the Armies of Tiglath-Pileser III and Sargon II, Stephanie Dalley, Iraq, Vol. 47 (1985), pp. 31-48
https://www.nationalgeographic.co.uk/history-and-civilisation/2020/05/hittites-fast-war-chariots-threatened-mighty-egypt
https://www.historynet.com/battle-of-kadesh.
http://dictionary.sensagent.com/Nisean%20horse/en-en/
https://www.horseoftheamericas.com/TheyHuntedTigers.htm
https://www.shorthistory.org/ancient-civilizations/mesopotamia/persian-empire/the-term-persia-and-medes-empire/
Horses_of_Different_Breeds_Observations.pdf Pauline ALBENDA New York
https://dailyhellas.com/2019/10/21/ancient-greco-chinese-war-of-the-heavenly-horses/
The Royal Horse of Europe: The Story of the Andalusian and Lusitano; Sylvia Loch, J.A. Allen, 1986
History of Horse Breeding, Daphne Machin Goodall, January 1, 1977
https://erenow.net/ancient/the-horse-the-wheel-and-language/16.php steppes
https://saberandscroll.weebly.com/uploads/1/1/7/9/11798495/5.2._a5.pdf steppes
https://www.nationalgeographic.com/animals/mammals/facts/przewalskis-horse
https://www.edgekz.com/kazakh-steppe-land-horse-tamed/
http://www.essential-humanities.net/world-history/steppe/ mongols
https://www.magnaceltae.com/post/ancient-celtic-warfare celts
https://www.artbycrane.com/horse_breeds/pony_breeds/garrano.htmltps://ihearthorses.com/exmoor-p http://www.legendsandchronicles.com/ancient-civilizations/ancient-rome/ancient-roman-class-structure/ony/
https://hadrianswallcountry.co.uk/learning/ideas-and-inspiration/hadrians-cavalry/cavalry-horses
https://www.reddit.com/r/AskHistorians/comments/2mrsps/were_horses_smaller_in_ancient_times_namely/
https://www.ancient.eu/Roman_Empire/
http://www.britannia.com/history/biographies/ambros.html
https://www.heroicage.org/issues/4/Hunter-Mann.html
https://www.archaeology.co.uk/articles/specials/timeline/sutton-hoo.htm

https://www.britannica.com/topic/Hengist
https://www.nationaltrust.org.uk/sutton-hoo/features/the-royal-burial-mounds-at-sutton-hoo
http://www.spiegel.de/international/europe/the-anglo-saxon-invasion-britain-is-more-germanic-than-it-thinks-a-768706-2.html
https://www.historic-uk.com/HistoryUK/HistoryofBritain/Invaders/
https://www.ancient.eu/Vortigern/
https://www.uni-due.de/SHE/HE_GermanicInvasions.htm
http://www.thenagain.info/WebChron/WestEurope/AngloSaxon.html
https://www.ourmigrationstory.org.uk/oms/anglo-saxon-migrations
http://www.thefinertimes.com/Middle-Ages/christianity-in-the-middle-ages.html
https://www.heritage-history.com/index.php?c=read&author=harding&book=middle&story=monastery
http://cowboyfrank.net/fortvalley/breeds/Andalusian.htm
https://www.ducksters.com/history/middle_ages_monastery.php
http://www.dallasequestriancenter.com/medieval-horse-breeds/
http://www.spanishvisionfarm.com/Articles/Bloodlines/bloodline_all_about_cartujano.html
http://www.thefinertimes.com/Middle-Ages/christianity-in-the-middle-ages.html
http://www.vlib.us/medieval/lectures/franks_rise.html
https://www.penfield.edu/webpages/jgiotto/onlinetextbook.cfm?subpage=1680226
https://www.britannica.com/biography/Roderick
https://www.history.com/topics/middle-ages/charles-martel-repels-the-moors-video
https://www.historyhit.com/day-charles-martel-dies/
https://www.reddit.com/r/AskHistorians/comments/345ito/when_did_england_become_britain/
https://www.historyextra.com/period/medieval/battle-hastings-facts-where-why-weapons-casualties-how-won/
http://www.lordsandladies.org
http://www.thearma.org/essays/pell/pellhistory.htm
https://www.abdn.ac.uk/sll/disciplines/english/lion/training.shtml
https://mad.hypotheses.org/375
https://stores.renstore.com/history-and-biography/horses-in-the-middle-ages
http://www.ox.ac.uk/news/2017-04-18-highs-and-lows-englishman%E2%80%99s-average-height-over-2000-years-0
http://www.localhistories.org/middle.html
http://www.equest4truth.com/94-discover-equus/159-horses-of-medieval-europe
http://www.medieval-life-and-times.info/medieval-life/medieval-hawking.htm

https://stores.renstore.com/history-and-biography/hors-in-the-middle-ages
https://www.alansfactoryoutlet.com/horses-in-the-middle-ages
https://www.warhistoryonline.com/medieval/11-facts-never-knew-medieval-warhorses.html
http://defendingcrusaderkingdoms.blogspot.com/2015/05/crusader-horses-destriers-palfreys-and.html
http://livingthehistoryelizabethchadwick.blogspot.com/2009/02/horses-for-courses.html
http://www.thefinertimes.com/Middle-Ages/tournaments-in-the-middle-ages.html
http://www.medievalchronicles.com/medieval-knights/medieval-tournaments/
https://www.thoughtco.com/the-holy-land-1788974
https://www.thevintagenews.com/2017/04/14/off-to-the-holy-places-pilgrimages-during-the-middle-ages/
http://www.internationalschooltoulouse.net/vs/pilgrims/motive.htm
https://www.haaretz.com/jewish/.premium-1009-the-mad-caliph-attacks-christian-sites-in-fatimid-empire-1.5450335
https://fogandfriction.com/2015/03/23/for-want-of-horses-and-ships-social-and-economic-constraints-of-christian-and-muslim-forces-during-the-third-crusade/
http://www.bbc.co.uk/history/historic_figures/richard_i_king.shtml
https://www.angus-donald.com/history/king-richards-return-imprisonment-and-ransom/
http://www.themiddleages.net/people/richard_lionheart.html
https://www.historyextra.com/period/medieval/robin-hood-real-myths-facts/
https://www.storiestogrowby.org/story/robin-hood-and-the-golden-arrow-story-legend-stories-for-kids/
http://afe.easia.columbia.edu/mongols/china/china.htm
https://asiasociety.org/education/mongol-dynasty
https://www.history.com/topics/china/genghis-khan
https://www.historyonthenet.com/the-mongol-empires-best-weapon-the-mongolian-horse
https://www.sapiens.org/column/off-the-map/horse-domestication-mongolia/
https://www.petguide.com/breeds/horse/mongolian-horse/
http://afe.easia.columbia.edu/mongols/conquests/khans_horses.pdf
https://www.degruyter.com/downloadpdf/j/apd.2018.6.issue-1/apd-2018-0003/apd-2018-0003.pdf
http://steventill.com/2008/06/18/the-diffusion-of-the-stirrup-into-medieval-western-europe/
The Medieval Horse and Its Equipment, C.1150-c.1450 edited by John Clark

Oakeshott, Ewart (1998) A Knight and His Horse. Rev. 2nd Ed. USA:Dufour Editions ISBN 0-8023-1297-7 Clark, John (Ed) (2004) The Medieval Horse and its Equipment: c. 1150-c. 1450. Rev. 2nd Ed, UK: The Boydell Press ISBN 1-84383-097-3

http://horsehints.org/MiddleAgesHorse.htm
https://www.metmuseum.org/art/collection/search/25452
https://www.paulickreport.com/horse-care-category/hoof-care-category/evolution-horse-breeding-domestication-affected-horse-genome/
https://cartujano-pre.de/en/cartujano/die-pferdezucht-philipps-ii/
http://www.trakehners-international.com/history/index.html
https://www.horsebreedspictures.com/holsteiner-horse.asp
https://www.horsebreedspictures.com/hanoverian-horse.asp
https://www.horsebreedspictures.com/oldenburg-horse.asp
https://www.horsebreedspictures.com/friesian-horse.asp
http://friesian-equine.co.uk/history-of-friesian-horse.html
https://www.countrylife.co.uk/out-and-about/sporting-country-pursuits/shetlands-shires-native-horse-breeds-britain-91125
https://www.historyextra.com/period/medieval/6-things-you-probably-didnt-know-about-the-ottoman-empire/
https://www.history.com/topics/middle-east/ottoman-empire
http://www.theottomans.org/english/family/osman.asp
https://www.encyclopedia.com/people/history/middle-eastern-history-biographies/osman-i
https://www.realmofhistory.com/2018/06/19/facts-ottoman-janissaries/
https://searchinginhistory.blogspot.com/2015/02/sipahi-heavy-weight-of-ottoman-empire.html
https://nzhistory.govt.nz/media/photo/ottoman-mamluk-cavalryman
http://www.hurriyetdailynews.com/the-ottomans-and-their-love-of-horses-65556
https://www.volkansadventures.com/history/brief-history-turkish-horse/
http://www.museumofthehorse.org/a-look-at-the-turkoman-horse-in-iran/
https://www.deseretnews.com/article/865580842/This-week-in-history-The-Fall-of-Constantinople-had-profound-consequences.html
https://quatr.us/medieval/late-medieval-russia-history.htm
https://www.biography.com/people/ivan-the-terrible-9350679
https://www.ducksters.com/history/middle_ages/kievan_rus.php
https://www.britannica.com/biography/Ivan-III
http://factsanddetails.com/russia/History/sub9_1b/entry-4935.html
https://www.realmofhistory.com/2018/08/29/facts-cossacks-don-zaporozhian/
https://www.history-magazine.com/cossacks.html
https://www.quora.com/How-do-Ivan-the-Great-and-Ivan-the-Terrible-differ
https://www.biography.com/people/ivan-the-terrible-9350679

https://www.flamesofwar.com/Default.aspx?tabid=112&art_id=696&kb_cat_id=34
http://www.equiworld.net/breeds/don/index.htm
https://www.ducksters.com/history/middle_ages/hundred_years_war.php
https://www.historyextra.com/period/medieval/7-facts-about-the-hundred-years-war/
https://www.bbc.com/news/magazine-28161434
https://www.historyextra.com/period/medieval/the-black-prince-hero-or-villain/
https://www.warhistoryonline.com/medieval/land-forces-hundred-years-war-mm.html
https://www.theguardian.com/childrens-books-site/2015/oct/25/battle-of-agincourt-600th-anniversary-linda-davies
https://www.historylearningsite.co.uk/medieval-england/the-longbow/
https://www.history.com/topics/british-history/wars-of-the-roses
https://www.history.com/topics/british-history/henry-viii
https://yesterday.uktv.co.uk/history/classic-history/kings-and-queens/article/tudors-1485-1603/
https://www.tudorsociety.com/8320-2/#more-8320
https://www.theanneboleynfiles.com/resources/q-a/did-henry-viii-either-have-his-own-horse-or-a-favourite/
http://www.tudorhorse.com/
http://myths.e2bn.org/mythsandlegends/origins1-humpty-dumpty-and-the-fall-of-colchester.html
https://www.british-history.ac.uk/office-holders/vol11/pp603-604
https://www.onlinebetting.org.uk/betting-guides/horse-racing/history-of-horse-racing.html
https://glreview.org/article/article-677/
https://www.horseracing.co.uk/history/british-racing/
http://www.newmarketshops.info/James_I_&_Charles_I_Palace.html
http://www.olivercromwell.org/newmarket.htm
https://www.encyclopedia.com/history/encyclopedias-almanacs-transcripts-and-maps/rise-monarchies-france-england-and-spain
https://www.history.com/topics/inventions/printing-press
https://worldhistory.us/european-history/the-rise-of-nationalism-during-the-renaissance.php
https://www.historylearningsite.co.uk/france-in-the-sixteenth-century/louis-xi/
http://american_almanac.tripod.com/louisxi.htm
http://www.sdopera.com/Content/Operapaedia/Operas/Rigoletto/FrancisIofFrance.htm
https://en.wikipedia.org/wiki/Grand_Squire_of_France
http://countrystudies.us/spain/7.htm

https://www.bartleby.com/essay/The-Accomplishments-of-Queen-Isabella-and-King-PK7SSJ6SWGDSX
https://web.archive.org/web/20141217041847/http://www.ialha.org/our-breed-2/how-andalusians-friesians-lipizzaners-and-lusitanos-are-called-baroque-horses/
http://theborgias.wikifoundry.com/page/POWERFUL+FAMILIES+of+Renaissance+Italy
https://www.ducksters.com/history/renaissance/italian_city-states.php
https://myarmoury.com/feature_armies_italy.html
https://en.wikipedia.org/wiki/Neapolitan_horse
https://www.britannica.com/biography/Charles-V-Holy-Roman-emperor
https://www.chronofhorse.com/article/history-spanish-riding-school-vienna
https://www.britannica.com/place/Vienna/History
https://www.history.com/topics/reformation/martin-luther-and-the-95-theses
https://www.historytoday.com/archive/charles-v%E2%80%99s-spanish-abdication
https://en.wikipedia.org/wiki/Charles_II,_Archduke_of_Austria
http://www.lipizzanconnection.com/history/
http://www.lipizzan.org/aboutlipizzans.html
https://www.tempelfarms.com/the-history-of-the-lipizzan.html
https://dailyhistory.org/What_was_the_role_of_the_Popes_in_the_Renaissance%3F
https://www.artofmanliness.com/articles/man-knowledge-the-basics-of-art-the-renaissance/
https://www.thoughtco.com/age-of-exploration-1435006
https://www.mrnussbaum.com/explorers/princehenry/
https://www.ducksters.com/biography/explorers/ferdinand_magellan.php
http://www.imh.org/exhibits/online/legacy-of-the-horse/colonial-horses/
http://www.newenglandhistoricalsociety.com/narragansett-pacer-lost-horse-new-england-colonies/
http://articles.mcall.com/1988-03-06/entertainment/2614046_1_five-horses-conestoga-breed
http://afs.okstate.edu/breeds/horses/morgan/index.html
https://en.wikipedia.org/wiki/Morgan_horse

Revolotionary Times
http://www.taxhistory.org/www/website.nsf/Web/THM1756?OpenDocument
http://philadelphiaencyclopedia.org/archive/horses/
https://www.paulreverehouse.org/the-real-story/
http://www.revolutionarywararchives.org/cavalry.html
http://www.equitrekking.com/articles/entry/sybil-ludington-and-her-horse-star-heroes-of-the-american-revolution/

https://www.encyclopediavirginia.org/Jack_Jouett_s_Ride_1781
https://www.awesomestories.com/asset/view/The-Horse-America-Throwing-His-Master-1779-Cartoon
https://www.thehistorycat-us.com/the-american-revolution
https://www.stratfordhall.org/meet-the-lee-family/henry-lee-iii/
https://www.u-s-history.com/pages/h1294.html

Advancing Frontier
http://www.lewis-clark.org/article/3342
https://truewestmagazine.com/the-mormon-handcart-migration/
https://www.farmcollector.com/farm-life/making-american-plow
http://www.historynet.com/mormon-handcart-horrors.htm
http://kentuckyancestors.org/the-untraveled-history-of-the-wilderness-road/
http://www.wondersandmarvels.com/2015/09/why-i-fell-in-love-with-sarah-royce-pioneer-woman-of-the-gold-rush.html
https://nationalponyexpress.org/historic-pony-express-trail/founders/
http://amhistory.si.edu/ourstory/activities/sodhouse/more.html
http://www.lrgaf.org/articles/ahta.htm
http://plainshumanities.unl.edu/encyclopedia/doc/egp.gen.040

Civil War
http://ushistoryscene.com/article/civilwaranimals/
http://www.thomaslegion.net/americancivilwar/totalcivilwarhorseskilled.html
http://www.civilwar.com/overview/315-weapons/148532-cavalry-62478.html
https://civilwar.mrdonn.org/supplytrains.html
https://www.civilwarhorses.net/links.php?326695
http://www.civil-war.net/cw_images/files/images/367.jpg
http://www.loc.gov/teachers/classroommaterials/presentationsandactivities/presentations/timeline/riseind/city
https://www.earthintransition.org/2013/02/horses-in-the-civil-war/
https://www.youtube.com/watch?v=qLbVPjxqlZ0 11th Ohio Volunteer Cavalry

Growth of Cities/WWI/On the Move
https://ephemeralnewyork.wordpress.com/2012/01/24/the-horse-walks-hiding-in-greenwich-village/
https://ephemeralnewyork.wordpress.com/2012/12/08/lovely-fountains-for-city-horses-and-other-animals/
https://ephemeralnewyork.wordpress.com/2016/06/30/the-1904-horse-auction-house-in-the-east-village/
http://mentalfloss.com/article/83608/10-relics-horse-powered-city
https://www.sfmta.com/getting-around/muni/cable-cars/cable-car-history

http://www.foundsf.org/index.php?title=The_Heyday_of_Horsecars
https://courses.lumenlearning.com/ushistory2os2xmaster/chapter/urbanization-and-its-challenges/
https://theblobologist.wordpress.com/2013/05/12/horsepower/
https://www.horsetalk.co.nz/2014/02/17/how-equine-flu-brought-us-standstill/
https://blogs.loc.gov/picturethis/2015/10/work-horses-pulling-their-weight/
http://frozen61.tripod.com/id5.html
https://www.carriageassociationofamerica.com/coson-carriage-tour/gigs-carts/
https://www.carriageassociationofamerica.com/carriage-tour/stanhope-gig/
https://www.thehenryford.org/collections-and-research/digital-collections/artifact/27990
https://www.pantagraph.com/news/local/great-epizootic-of-brought-commerce-to-a-standstill/article_a7f6135b-6803-5018-aeb5-a8003f8b9759.html
https://fee.org/articles/the-great-horse-manure-crisis-of-1894/
https://www.rtbf.be/ww1/topics/detail_the-horse-an-essential-participant-of-the-great-war?id=8358614)
https://www.nap.edu/read/4980/chapter/2#15
https://thetyee.ca/News/2013/03/06/Horse-Dung-Big-Shift/
https://parkcityhistory.org/wp-content/uploads/2012/04/Teacher-Background-Information.pdf

America Today
http://www.horsecouncil.org/press-release/ahcf-announces-results-2017-economic-impact-study/
https://www.fei.org/stories/weg-2018-disciplines-explained
https://www.uspolo.org/sport/rules
https://www.washingtonpost.com/news/style/wp/2018/02/22/feature/will-a-new-generation-save-fox-hunting/?utm_term=.d73218e73dff
https://www.crchealth.com/types-of-therapy/what-is-equine-therapy/
https://www.breyerhorses.com/breyer_history

Purposeful Breeding
https://thehorse.com/112805/responsible-purposeful-horse-breeding/
https://www.pval.org/cms/lib/NY19000481/Centricity/Domain/86/horse%20book%20chapter.pdf
http://afs.okstate.edu/breeds/horses/thoroughbred/index.html thoroughbred
https://www.localriding.com/origin-of-the-thoroughbred-horse.html/3 thoroughbred

Biomehanics

https://aaep.org/sites/default/files/issues/proceedings-08proceedings-z9100108000001.PDF p 3 -4
https://equineink.com/2019/08/10/the-stages-of-equine-skeletal-development/?fbclid=IwAR3qZBfq739wjMJCzW22GA9tzCmHRTN-8hafK56rdYFlzt4pDaxcExlEhqfs#:~:text=The%20last%20bones%20to%20fuse,they%20are%208%20(source) growth rate
https://archive.org/details/pointsofhorsetre00haye excellent old book
https://www.amazon.com/Tug-War-Classical-Incorrect-Negatively/dp/1570763755
https://www.amazon.com/Balancing-Act-Sport-Irreconcilable-Conflict/dp/1646010728/ref=pd_sbs_2?pd_rd_w=6bOM7&pf_rd_p=2419a049-62bf-452e-b0d0-ca5b7e35a7b4&pf_rd_r=21YZ8FHP9W2V2Y-CKY1Z5&pd_rd_r=b29a3622-71ee-4ec7-b7ee-2c2f5fcf478d&pd_rd_wg=rTdV9&pd_rd_i=1646010728&psc=1
https://horsesport.com/magazine/health/dressage-conformation/
https://www.swannequineosteo.com/blog/2017/12/5/equine-biomechanics-research-the-significance-of-a-horses-chest-sling-muscles
https://animalcorner.org/horse-anatomy/
https://coherenthorsemanship.com/2020/08/11/comparative-anatomy/
https://murdochmethod.com/comparable-parts-you-are-more-like-your-horse-than-you-think/
https://extension.umn.edu/horse-care-and-management/conformation-horse
https://animalrangeextension.montana.edu/equine/locomotion.html
https://scitechdaily.com/extra-gaits-in-horses-traced-to-single-mutation/
https://www.helpfulhorsehints.com/what-is-a-gaited-horse/
https://practicalhorsemanmag.com/training/evaluating-horse-form-function-31701
https://jumpernation.com/sport-horse-conformation-shoulders/ jumper conformation
https://www.behindthebitblog.com/2008/06/dressage-versus-jumper-conformation.html jumper and dressage conformation
https://equestrianism.wordpress.com/2008/07/21/jumper-conformation/ jumper conformation
https://horsesport.com/magazine/health/dressage-conformation/
https://www.swannequineosteo.com/blog/2017/12/5/equine-biomechanics-research-the-significance-of-a-horses-chest-sling-muscles self carriage
https://www.horseracing.com/blog/conformation-of-a-racehorse/ racing
http://www.favourstud.com/images/Conformation.pdf racing
https://practicalhorsemanmag.com/health-archive/whats-the-ideal-endurance-horse-conformation endurance
https://melnewton.com/2015/the-way-i-see-it/ endurance

https://equinehusbandry.ces.ncsu.edu/wp-content/uploads/2015/02/Conformation-of-the-American-Saddlebred.pdf?fwd=no

https://www.youtube.com/watch?v=N8cSY-SHBpA Larry Trocha performance horse analysis

https://www.horsejournals.com/riding-training/more-disciplines/trail/trail-tips-conformation-trail-horse trail/packing

https://www.horsejournals.com/trimming-shoeing/good-hoof-bad-hoof

https://www.horseracing.com/blog/buying-and-owning-a-standardbred/

https://www.thehorseguide.com/horse-breed-information/warm-blood-breeds/standardbred/

https://allaboutstandardbreds.blogspot.com/2009/07/standardbred-breeding-whats-in.html

http://www.spphav.org.au/index.php?page=the-standardbred

https://horserookie.com/how-much-weight-can-a-horse-pull/ work horse

https://thehorse.com/194403/built-to-last-ideal-equine-conformation/

https://www.equestrianandhorse.com/draft/breeds.html

https://en.wikipedia.org/wiki/Show_jumping

https://en.wikipedia.org/wiki/Dressage

https://en.wikipedia.org/wiki/Endurance_riding

Temperament

https://horsewhorls.com/

https://www.pathintl.org/63-resources/resources-landing-page/1441-equine-tips-evaluating-horse-temperament-personality

https://www.besthorserider.com/horse-temperament-scale/

https://equipedia.ifce.fr/fileadmin/bibliotheque/7.Technical_information/The-horse-s-temperament.pdf

https://bjbas.springeropen.com/articles/10.1186/s43088-021-00133-8

Image Sources

1 "Richard III, King of England, Uncle of Elizabeth of York, Great Uncle of Henry VIII" by lisby1 is marked with CC PDM . By Ann Longmore-Etheridge - https://www.flickr.com/photos/60861613@N00/15476633186/, CC BY-SA 4.0, https://commons.wikimedia.org/w/index.php?curid=112268255

2 A gallic-roman harvester. Relief from Trier. Public Domain, https://commons.wikimedia.org/w/index.php?curid=1717542

3 Ashurbanipal II hunts wild asses, on a horseback. Alabaster-bas relief. From Room S, North Palace at Nineveh, Iraq, 645-635 BCE. British Museum, London. By Osama Shukir Muhammed Amin FRCP(Glasg) - Own work, CC BY-SA 4.0, https://commons.wikimedia.org/w/index.php?curid=105667448

4 A series of skulls and feet. Eohippus, Mesohippus, Meryhippus, Hipparion and Equus. American Museum of Natural History. By Thomas Hunt Morgan - A Critique of the Theory of Evolution., available freely at Project Gutenberg, Public Domain, https://commons.wikimedia.org/w/index.php?curid=12724483

5 These two maps viewed from the North Pole at early and mid-Late Cretaceous, which illustrates the formation of Bering Land Bridge between Asia and North America. By JacqCLSin - Own work, CC BY-SA 4.0, https://commons.wikimedia.org/w/index.php?curid=83741318

6 Midern View of Equid Evolution. Addison wesley Longman, Inc. Copyright 1999. https://www.mun.ca/biology/scarr/Equid_evolution_Campbell.htm

7 The rare three-toed Dawn Horse fossil discovered by Jim Tynsky in his quarry in the Green River Formation near Kemmerer. Tynsky's rare fossil is prepared and packed for delivery to the Smithsonian Museum of Natural History in D.C. https://kemmerergazette.com/article/from-kemmerer-to-washington-dc

8 A fully articulated primitive horse ancestor, since nicknamed "Olive", was found by brothers Mark and Mike Oliver. https://www.fossilera.com/pages/new-fossil-discovery-olive-a-primitive-horse-ancestor-from-the-green-river-formation

9 Graph by Equine Heritage Institute. Illustration, skull and leg bones found at - Explore the fascinating evolutionary journey of the modern horse - https://equineguelph.ca/learn_objects/evolutiontimeline/timeline.html

10 D.E. MacHugh et al/Annu. Rev. Anim. Biosci. 2017; M. Germonpré et al/J. Archaeol. Sci. 2009

11 Emperor Caligula on horseback. By Rijksmuseum - http://hdl.handle.net/10934/RM0001.COLLECT.96856, CC0, https://commons.wikimedia.org/w/index.php?curid=85412304

12 Image of a horse from the Lascaux caves. By Own work, Public Domain, https://commons.wikimedia.org/w/index.php?curid

13 Chase Hunt. By Unknown author - http://tpmcafe.talkingpointsmemo.com/talk/blogs/quinn_esq/2009/09/head-smashed-inbuffalo-jump.php, Public Domain, https://commons.wikimedia.org/w/index.php?curid=8010440

14 Head-Smashed-In Buffalo Jump. By <ahref="//commons.wikimedia.org/w/index.php?title=User:Lazarus000&action=edit&redlink=1"class="new" title="User:Lazarus000 (page does not exist)">Lazarus000</a> - <span class="int-ownwork" lang="en">Own work</span>, <ahref="https://creativecommons.org/licenses/by-sa/4.0" title="Creative Commons Attribution-Share Alike 4.0">CC BY-SA 4.0</a>, <a href="https://commons.wikimedia.org/w/index.php?curid=45659978">Link</a>pg 22 - Head-Smashed-In Buffalo Jump. By

183

Carol M. Highsmith - Library of CongressCatalog: http://lccn.loc.gov/2015634147Image download: https://cdn.loc.gov/master/pnp/highsm/34100/34131a.tifOriginal url: http://hdl.loc.gov/loc.pnp/highsm.34131, Public Domain, https://commons.wikimedia.org/w/index.php?curid=51492972 Public Domain, https://commons.wikimedia.org/w/index.php?curid=227766

15 Rope Making tool. https://www.livescience.com/59756-oldest-ropestools-unearthed.html

16 Neolithic Village. https://pixabay.com/photos/village-neolithicancient-1513507/

17 Skara Brae Neolithic Village. https://www.ancient-scotland.co.uk/site/skara-brae-neolithic-village

18 Chariot drawn by bulls. By Zde - Own work, CC BY-SA 4.0, https://commons.wikimedia.org/w/index.php?curid=53060019

19 Clay chariot model, beginning of the 2nd millennium B.C, Musée du Louvre

20 The Standard of Ur. By Unknown author - "Royal Standard of Ur" - Mosaic With Sumer Images, Awesome Stories., Public Domain, https://commons.wikimedia.org/w/index.php?curid=458495

21 Kikkuli text. By Osama Shukir Muhammed Amin FRCP(Glasg) - Own work, CC BY-SA 4.0, https://commons.wikimedia.org/w/index.php?curid=94644325

22 Ancient Measurements - Relief of Ninfi, between Sardis and Smyrna. Book. The history of Herodotus. A new English version, ed. with copious notes and appendices, illustrating the history and geography of Herodotus, from the most recent sources of information; and embodying the chief results, historical and ethnographical, which have been obtained in the progress of cuneiform and hieroglyphical discovery. 1862. Authors: Herodotus Rawlinson, George, 1812-1902 Rawlinson, Henry Creswicke, Sir, 1810-1895 Wilkinson, John Gardner, Sir, 1797-1875

23 Francesco Faraone Aquila, Statue group of Alexander and Bucephalus, 1704, engraving, British Museum.

24 Richard Stone Reeves is considered to be the 20th century's premier racing portraitist and perhaps the most important American painter of sporting art ever. Known for his accuracy and realism, Reeves' ability to capture the personality and character of each subject was legendary. In 1970, Reeves, was commissioned by the Thoroughbred Record magazine to paint "The Perfect Horse". In this work; the artist used Tie Polleto's head and neck, Citation's shoulder, Jay Trump's forelegs, Vaguely Nobel's middle piece, Buck Passer's quarters and hindlimbs, and Graustark's color. In his description of "The Perfect Horse," he stated that "all the horses were top class runners indeed

25 Monique and Hans D Dossenbach (Collins, Sydney 1986) https://agecroft.wordpress.com/ancient-breeds-of-horse/

26 Monique and Hans D Dossenbach (Collins, Sydney 1986) https://agecroft.wordpress.com/ancient-breeds-of-horse/

27 Early societies which bred horses. "A History of Horse Breeding" by Daphne Machin Goodall

28 The elaborate panels at the southern end of the Apadana staircase in Persepolis are a record of nations, The panels show 23 delegations bringing their gifts to the Achaemenid king, Darius the Great (522-486 BC.) The Ethiopians begin the frieze in the bottom left corner and are joined by Arabs, Thracians, Kasmiris, Parthians and Cappadocians. The Elamites, Egyptians and Medians occupy the

panel at top right. Note the size of horses.

29 Sorraia horse. https://www.horsebreedsinfo.com/Sorraia-pictures,-video,-and-information.html

30 Arabian horse. Lithograph by Otto Eerelmand and Rich. Schoenbeck. Gloria Austin Collection

31 Numidia. https://fmarcosmarin.blogspot.com/2015/05/un-mito-etnolinguistico-la-palabra-moro.html

32 Berber horse. Lithograph by Otto Eerelmand and Rich. Schoenbeck. Gloria Austin Collection.

33 Iberian horse. By After Abraham van Diepenbeeck - Welbeck Le Superbe Cheval de Spanie at beinecke.library.yale.edu, Public Domain, https://commons.wikimedia.org/w/index.php?curid=4532087

34 The Steppes. https://www.britannica.com/place/the-Steppe

35 Mongolian Archer - By Muhammad ibn Mahmudshah al-Khayyam - http://www.lacma.org/khan/5/6.htm archive copy, Public Domain, https://commons.wikimedia.org/w/index.php?curid=1623743

36 Mongolian horses today. https://www.petguide.com/breeds/horse/mongolian-horse/

37 Chariots, Standard of Ur War panel - By Unknown author - "Royal Standard of Ur" - Mosaic With Sumer Images, Awesome Stories., Public Domain, https://commons.wikimedia.org/w/index.php?curid=458495

38 Standard of Ur Peace Panel - By LeastCommonAncestor - Own work, CC BY-SA 3.0, https://commons.wikimedia.org/w/index.php?curid=33038063

39 Epitaph stelae (tomb inscription) depicting a horse.

40 Gravestone in Mycenae from 1500 BC - thought to be one of the oldest pictures of a chariot from that area.

41 Sacraficed horse. By Schuppi - Own work, CC BY-SA 4.0, https://commons.wikimedia.org/w/index.php?curid=95713939

42 Two Ladies: Tiryns. By Gary Todd from Xinzheng, China - Mycenaean Fresco of Tiryns, CC0, https://commons.wikimedia.org/w/index.php?curid=109052626

43 Two Ladies: Hagia Triada. By ArchaiOptix - Own work, CC BY-SA 4.0, https://commons.wikimedia.org/w/index.php?curid=90755793

44 Metope Centaur at Athens Acropolis Museum. By Ad MeskensYou are free to use this picture for any purpose as long as you credit its author, Ad Meskens.Example: © Ad Meskens / Wikimedia CommonsIf you use this work outside of the Wikimedia projects, a message or a copy is very much appreciated.This image is not in the public domain. A statement such as "-From Wikimedia Commons" or similar is not by itself sufficient. If you do not provide clear attribution to the author you didn't comply with the terms of the file's license and may not use this file. If you are unable or unwilling to provide attribution you should contact Ad Meskens to negotiate a different license.This file has been released under a license which is incompatible with Facebook's licensing terms. It is not permitted to upload this file to Facebook. - Own work, CC BY-SA 4.0, https://commons.wikimedia.org/w/index.php?curid=85092668

45 Mycenaean Gold Signet Ring, Aidonia, 1500 BC. By Zde - Own work, CC BY-SA 4.0, https://commons.wikimedia.org/w/index.php?curid=99577872

46 Bucephalus & Alexander https://wall.alphacoders.com/big.php?i=346779

47 Modern Pindos Pony https://historandmor.blogspot.com/2016/08/the-thessalian-cavalry.html

48 Ancient coinage of Thessaly, By Johny SYSEL - Own work, CC BY-SA 3.0, https://commons.

185

wikimedia.org/w/index.php?curid=28874395

49 The small size of the horse can easily be seen , in relation to the riders, depicted on the frieze and pottery of the region. By Unknown artist - Jastrow (2006), Public Domain, https://commons.wikimedia.org/w/index.php?curid=1423323

50 The Trojan horse - S. G. Goodrich Lights and Shadows of European History (Boston: Bradbury, Soden, & Co., 1844) 40

51 Greek horseman, 3rd Century BC. By This file was donated to Wikimedia Commons as part of a project by the Metropolitan Museum of Art. See the Image and Data Resources Open Access Policy, CC0, https://commons.wikimedia.org/w/index.php?curid=60416861

52 Battle of Kadesh - https://poiopoio.blogspot.com/2012/01/movilizacion-general-en-la-antiguedad.html

53 Egyptian Chariot, Scanned from Nineveh and Its Palaces, by Joseph Bonomi, figure 10, 1853. By Joseph Bonomi - Scanned from Nineveh and Its Palaces, by Joseph Bonomi, figure 108, Public Domain, https://commons.wikimedia.org/w/index.php?curid=3199968

53a The Ketdkn of the north wall of the Hyposttlb Hall at Karnak, where Seti I. represents some episodes in his first campaign. And the Hittite king was absent in some other part of his empire. Photo from the book The Struggle of the nations - Egypt, Syria, and Assyria by Maspero, Gaston (1896).

54 Hittite chariot - By from Paul Volz: Die biblischen Altertümer (1914), p. 514. copied from de:Hethitischer Streitwagen.jpg., Public Domain, https://commons.wikimedia.org/w/index.php?curid=360357

54a War chariot; height : 175 cm; Carchemish ; second half of 8th c. BC; Late Hittite style under Assyro-Aramaean influence; Museum of Anatolian Civilizations, Ankara, Turkey. By Georges Jansoone (JoJan) - Self-photographed, CC BY-SA 3.0, https://commons.wikimedia.org/w/index.php?curid=2129173

55 Assyrian Empire 650 BC https://world-mapp.blogspot.com/2020/01/map-of-assyrian-empire-650-bc.html

56 Assyrian lion hunting relief from Nineveh, depicting grooms holding horses. Tag on exhibit reads: "Courtiers watching lion hunts. Assyrian, about 645-635 BC. From Nineveh, North Palace, Room S, panel 6, top and middle rows. WA 124882" See BM database entry for more details. By Ealdgyth (Own work), CC BY-SA 3.0, https://commons.wikimedia.org/w/index.php?curid=11046265

57 Assyrian military campaign in southern Mesopotamia, horses and palm trees, 7th century BC, from Nineveh

58 A Chinese walking Nisean (Tien' Ma) spotted horse with estimated firing date between 900-1500 years ago of Tang (618-906 AD) form , with thermoluminescence Analysis Report by Oxford Authentication Ltd. 21" approx. https://www.invaluable.com/auction-lot/a-chinese-walking-nisean-tien-ma-spotted-hor-43045228F7

59 The Kara-Khanid ruler Ilig Khan on horse submitting to Mahmud of Ghazni riding an elephant, Persian painting, 1306-14. By 14th century Persian painter - [1], Public Domain, https://commons.wikimedia.org/w/index.php?curid=113560130

60 Heavenly Horse. Ceremonial bronze finial with standing horse, 4th-1st century BC. This ceremonial bronze finial with standing horse is an artifact from the Greco-Bactrian Kingdom. As the Scythians came into contact with the Greeks in the Greco-Bactrian kingdom, artists from the two cultures influenced each other. The bronze finial has much in common with the famous Scythian gold artifacts found thousands of kilometers to the west on the banks of the Bosphorus and the Chersonese, although a high degree of cultural syncretism characterizes the bronze fini-

al. Hellenistic cultural and artistic influences can be seen in many aspects of the horse sculpture, which can be attributed to the existence of the Greco-Bactrian Kingdom. This demonstrates the richness of the cultural influences in the Bactria area at the time. The bronze horse has a refined head, a swan-like neck, a slim body, and a deep chest, and it is sitting atop the finial with its long legs stretched out. The artwork combines Scythian and Hellenistic elements. The horse's long mane is depicted in the Hellenistic style, while its ribs are presented in the anatomical style. During the Hellenistic period, the styles of sculptures ranged from the anatomical style to the naturalistic and realistic styles. An ancient Hellenistic pattern is also featured on the base of the finial. The bronze finial with horse is a clear example of the animal style of art. The animal style typical of Scythian culture is associated with a rich variety of plastics as well as the symmetry of composite solutions. Artifacts such as the finial were mounted on shafts and buildings for ritual purposes. The rulers of the Scythian commonly used finials for ceremonies dedicated to the cult of Heavenly Horses when traveling, attending festivals, and even horse racing. Archeologists and researchers have long been attracted to Scythian artworks due to their conventional stylization of details and appropriate elements. At the same time, such artworks demonstrate a high degree of accuracy and reflect the highly artistic approach of the Scythian animal style. The Scythian culture gave rise to artifacts that are now recognized as masterpieces of ancient art. The various representations of horses in these artworks indicate how important they were to Scythian culture. Artworks such as the bronze finial depict stronger and bigger horses, which reveals the presence of cross-breeding. After cross-breeding, the new horses were highly valued due to their graceful and elegant appearance. The breeders also valued animals that exhibited endurance and speed. These new horses have been described as being much faster and stronger than the typical Chinese and Mongolian horse breeds. Indeed, the "heavenly" horses were fast and light. Jonathan Tao, a research historian from the University of Chicago, author of Heavenly Horses of Bactria: The Creation of the Silk Road, has stated that the bronze finial should be identified with an ancestor of the modern Akhal-Teke horse breed, a descendant of the "heavenly horses" acquired from Central Asia during the War of the Heavenly Horses. The War of the Heavenly Horses (or the Han-Dayuan War) was a military conflict fought from 104 BC to 102 BC between the Chinese Han dynasty and the Scythian-ruled Dayuan which was part of the Greco-Bactrian Kingdom. The war was fought in the Ferghana Valley at the easternmost end of the former Persian Empire (between modern-day Uzbekistan, Kyrgyzstan, and Tajikistan). More specifically, Dayuan (or Tayuan; Chinese: ; pinyin: Dàyuān; literally: "Great Ionians") was a city-state in the Ferghana Valley in Central Asia, which is described in Chinese historical texts such as the Records of the Grand Historian and the Book of Han. It is also mentioned in accounts written by the famous Chinese explorer Zhang Qian and the numerous ambassadors who followed him into Central Asia in 130 BC. The Dayuan people were the descendants of Greek colonists who followed Alexander the Great and settled in Ferghana in 329 BC. They prospered within the Hellenistic realm of the Seleucids and Greco-Bactrians until they were isolated by the migration of the Scythian people in around 140 BC. It appears that the name "Yuan" was simply a transliteration of the Sanskrit terms "Yavana" or "Pali Yona," which were used throughout antiquity in Asia to designate Greeks (or Ionians). This indicates that "Dayuan" was used to refer to "Great Ionians" or "Great Greeks." By 100 BC, the Dayuan people had been defeated by the Han dynasty in the Han-Dayuan War. This interaction between the Dayuan people and the Chinese is historically crucial, as it represents one of the first major instances of contact between an urbanized Western civilization and the Chinese civilization. As such, it helped to pave the way for the development of the Silk Road, which linked the East and the West in terms of both material and cultural exchange from the 1st century BC through to the 15th century. Thus, the role of horses in the development of Chinese civilization is hugely significant. Due to understanding the strategic importance of horse breeding, the Han empire was able to continue the development of its civilization. Through the use of elite breeds of horses, the art of warfare was modernized, which made it possible to adequately respond to raids by neighboring nomadic civilizations. The significance of the role of the horse is clearly reflected in the works of art of the Han period. The bronze finial of the horse belongs to those times when Han began to spread its influence in the territory of Ancient Central Asia, where the nomadic civilization challenged them. It was necessary to obtain an important military and strategic resource – the best horses, ready to compete with the cavalry of nomads. Ferghana "heavenly" horses belong to one of the world's earliest known cultural breeds of race-horses, a fast and light Eastern type, perfectly suited for cavalry. They are the ancestors of all the best Asian horse breeds: Arabian, Turkmen (Akhal-Teke), and Kyrgyz. Even allowing for the inevitable cross-breeding experiments over centuries and the blending of bloodlines since the time of Herodotus, the Akhal-Teke horse breed has retained the main features described by historians since ancient times, of which the bronze finial is proof.

61 Dayuan or Tayuan https://commons.m.wikimedia.org/wiki/File:Ta-YuanMap.jpg#mw-jump-to-license

62 Ferghana horse by Giuseppe Castiglione, a Jessuit painter in the Chinese court - 1748 titled A Horse named Dawanliu.

63 A rubbing of an image of Ferghana horses (or "heavenly horses") discovered in a tomb dating back to the Han Dynasty period.

64 Sweating Blood Horse Coin cast during the Song Dynasty.

65 Exmoor ponies https://horselifeandlove.blogspot.com/2015/12/exmoor-ponies.html Chambers's encyclopedia; a dictionary of universal knowledge for the people (1871) By Internet Archive Book Images - https://www.flickr.com/photos/internetarchivebookimages/14580013829/ Source book page: https://archive.org/stream/chamberssencyclo07phil/chamberssencyclo-07phil#page/n698/mode/1up, No restrictions, https://commons.wikimedia.org/w/index.php?curid=43510553

66 Image of a horse from the Lascaux caves made by the Cro-Magnon peoples at their hunting route in the Stone age By Own work, Public Domain, https://commons.wikimedia.org/w/index.php?curid=1907853

67 Tribes and cities in Gaul at the time of Julius Caesar. Data for this map were retrieved from a map out of the book "Julius Caesar" written by Philip Freeman (ISBN 978-1-906217-69-3). By Citypeek - http://sharemap.org/runnerup/FranceGeospatial data sources:Open Street Map Data (ODbL) - http://www.openstreetmap.org/copyrightNORTAD - http://www.bts.gov/publications/north_american_transportation_atlas_data/Natural Earth - http://www.naturalearthdata.com/, CC BY-SA 3.0, https://commons.wikimedia.org/w/index.php?curid=23753854

68 Celtic museum in Hallein (Salzburg). Reconstruction of a Celtic chariot. By Wolfgang Sauber - Own work, CC BY-SA 3.0, https://commons.wikimedia.org/w/index.php?curid=7849626

69 Garrano pony https://www.horsebreedspictures.com/garrano.asp

70 Icelandic horse. Photo by Clay Bonnyman Evans https://claybonnymanevans.com/pony-packs-the-colorado-trail-a-journal/icelandicpony

71 Maps of Caesar's campaigns in Gaul. By first uploader User:Kirill Lokshin 03:23, 9 March 2006 (UTC) - http://www.dean.usma.edu/history/ The Department of History, United States Military Academy, Public Domain, https://commons.wikimedia.org/w/index.php?curid=35003356

72 The reconstructed Roman Eifel aqueduct near Mechernich, Germany. By Carole Raddato from FRANKFURT, Germany - The reconstructed Roman Eifel aqueduct near Mechernich, GermanyUploaded by Marcus Cyron, CC BY-SA 2.0, https://commons.wikimedia.org/w/index.php?curid=30161791

72a The remains of the barracks at Chesters Roman Fort - Hadrian's Wall. On a family day out, visit Chesters Roman Fort, built almost 2,000 years ago to house a Roman army garrison guarding the nearby bridge across the River Tyne. See a well-preserved strong room and military bathhouse and gain insight into what life would have been like for the men and horses. https://www.english-heritage.org.uk/visit/places/chesters-roman-fort-and-museum-hadrians-wall/history/absence-of-stables/

73 Mons(Var)Aqueduct from Mons to Fréjus partly rebuilt, home to the so-called modern springs (Laugier) By This illustration was made by (User:Royonx) and released under the license(s) stated above. You are free to use it for any purpose as long as you credit me and follow the terms of the license. Example : © Michel Royon / Wikimedia CommonsIf you use this image outside of the Wikimedia projects, I would be happy to hear from you par courriel (royonx gmail.com). Thanks !Ce message en français - Own work, CC BY-SA 3.0, https://commons.wikimedia.org/w/index.php?curid=3032289

74 Map - The Roman Empire 1st Century B.C. to A.D. 150. https://www.timemaps.com/history/europe-30bc/

75 Saint Robert's Journey. https://www.flickr.com/photos/saintrobert/199925709

76 Circus Maximus. https://someinterestingfacts.net/facts-circus-maximus-rome/

77 Incitatus https://www.schule-bw.de/faecher-und-schularten/gesellschaftswissenschaftliche-und-philosophische-faecher/geschichte/unterrichtsmaterialien/sekundarstufe-I/vorgeschantike/rom/caesarenwahn

78 Marcus Aurelius. https://smarthistory.org/equestrian-sculpture-of-marcus-aurelius/

79 Sketch of Przewalski's horse by Roborovsky. By Vsevolod Ivanovich Roborovsky (26 April 1856 – 23 July 1910) - V.I. Roborowsky, Public Domain, https://commons.wikimedia.org/w/index.php?curid=100314790

80 Equus gmelini - the Tarpan By ArtsCult.com - mammals-00027_-_TARPAN WILD HORSE [3124x1871]@G._1_01_, Public Domain, https://commons.wikimedia.org/w/index.php?curid=45635160

81 Equus europiums or Equus celticus, the plateau horse/ Exmoor pony. By Internet Archive Book Images - https://www.flickr.com/photos/internetarchivebookimages/14580013829/Source book page: https://archive.org/stream/chamberssencyclo07phil/chamberssencyclo07phil#page/n698/mode/1up, No restrictions, https://commons.wikimedia.org/w/index.php?curid=43510553

82 Cobb horse. By Théodore Géricault - http://www.relewis.com/gericaultcauchois.html, Public Domain, https://commons.wikimedia.org/w/index.php?curid=73304877

83 Equus orientalis - Arabian type, Caspian pony. Ancient writings and artefacts provide evidence that horses of the Caspian type existed as early as 3,000 BC. The British Museum has a terracotta plaque from second millennium BC Mesopotamia which depicts a small horse, ridden with a nose ring. During the Mongolian Wars, however, and again during the revolution in Iran, much of the documentation relating to the Caspian was destroyed. It is known that these horses were highly prized for ceremonial use, as well as for their agility. King Shapur (AD 260) and King Ardashir I (AD 224) are both shown on stone reliefs which depict small horses standing no more than waist high. Two horses of Caspian type were presented as gifts to King Darius the Great, as recorded on the stone staircase of the ancient Palace at Persepolis. The gift horses probably originated from Hamadan, where recent excavations revealed bones thought to be those of the early Caspian horse. More artefacts which form part of the Oxus Treasure show small horses of a similar type. Further proof of the . esteem in which the Caspian was held lies in the inclusion of this tiny horse on the royal seal of King Darius in 500 BC (see picture below). A king's fatness to rule was judged by his bravery and prowess at killing lions set loose in his Persian game park so, for the horses harnessed to his chariot, acceleration and agility was crucial. https://ca-za-caspian-stud.webnode.se/products/fleur-scott-/

189

84 Cheval de race barbe. By L. Moll & Eug. Gayot - Encyclopédie pratique de l'agriculteur, publiée par Firmin-Didot et Cie, tome 5, 1877, Public Domain, https://commons.wikimedia.org/w/index.php?curid=17353551

85 Rosie (once a member of Gloria Austin's 4-in-hand team) and Mary Chris Foxworthy in the arena.

86 "Right handed" knight. http://karenswhimsy.com/medieval-clipart.htm

87 Armor for man and horse by Kunz Lochner, Nuremberg, 1548. Horse armor belonged to Johann Ernst, Duke of Saxony. Photo by Michelle Lee. https://www.flickr.com/photos/michellerlee/7482507568/in/photostream/

88 Destriers horse. By Matthew Paris - Originally from en.wikipedia; description page is (was) here03:45, 26 March 2005 Dsmdgold 1565x762 (117701 bytes) ([[:en:William Marshall]] at a joust unhorses <a href="/w/index.php?title=Baldwin_Guisnes&action=edit" class="new" title="Baldwin Guisnes">Baldwin Guisnes]] in 1233. From the ''Historia Major'' of [[:en:Matthew Paris]], Cambridge, Corpus Christi College Library, vol 2, p. 85. Scanned from ''Four Gothic Kings'', Elizabeth Hallam, ed. {{PD-art}}), Public Domain, https://commons.wikimedia.org/w/index.php?curid=763562

89 Hawking or Falconry, The Devonshire Hunting Tapestries, late 1420s. Middle Ages: the beginning for hunting falcon, on horseback. Detail of a silk and wool tapestry from the beginning of the 16th century. From Hainaut. Paris, National Museum of the Middle Ages, Thermes de Cluny.

90 Rouncey on an illuminated manuscript, Romance of Alexander (Bodleian MS 264). folia's 96v and 73r in the marginalia. https://digital.bodleian.ox.ac.uk/objects/ae9f6cca-ae5c-4149-8fe4-95e6eca1f73c/

91 Chaucer's Wife of Bath rode a Palfrey seen in Canterbury Tales

92 Peasant Farmers. Simon Bening, Labors of the Months: September, from a Flemish Book of hours (Bruges) https://www.paintwalk.com/2020/06/dorset-heathland-history-2-middle-ages.html

93 A 13th Century farming scene: Le Régime des princes, 1279. https://britishfoodhistory.com/2017/07/13/mediaeval-feast-mediaeval-famine/

94 14th - 15th century litter at work during July. A Quiet Revolution – The Horse in Agriculture, 1100-1500. http://medieval.ucdavis.edu/20A/Villa.html

94a Farewell of Johann Frederick I of Saxony of Emperor Charles V, 16th century.

95 95 Lady in Horse-litter, returning from Tournament. 15th century. Harl, MS. 4431, Brit. Mus. Photo, Macbeth. Image facing page 132; from Of Six Mediæval Women, by Alice Kemp-Welch (1913) https://archive.org/details/ofsixmediaevalwo00kemprich/page/n191/mode/2up

96 Detail of a miniature of Ermengarda
in a carriage, with the castle and Pont de Fin of Lille, the giant Finard slaying Salvard, and Ermengarda received by the hermit. Netherlands, S. https://www.bl.uk/catalogues/illuminated-manuscripts/ILLUMIN.ASP?Size=mid&IllID=37695

97 Nonsuch Palace as seen in a hand-coloured engraving from Braun and Hogenberg's Civitates Orbis Terrarum, 1582 - Credit: Folger Shakespeare Library (CC BY-SA 2.0). https://www.greatbritishlife.co.uk/homes-and-gardens/places-to-live/henry-viii-and-surrey-history-7090038

98 St. George - by Raphael (Raffaello Sanzio da Urbino) between 1503 and 1505, Paris, France. https://www.raphaelpaintings.org/st-george.jsp

99 St. Geroge and the dragon. Miniature of St George and the Dragon, ms. of Legenda Aurea, dated 1348, BNF Français 241, fol. 101v.

100 Ottoman mail and plate armor for horse. Rider and horse armor from Mamluk Egypt (circa 1550), Musée de l'Armée, Paris. By Mohatatou - Own work, CC BY-SA 4.0, https://commons.wikime-

dia.org/w/index.php?curid=73562972

101 Russian Cossacks on horseback, circa 1900

102 King Henry VIII followed by Sir Anthony Brown, Master of the Horse. From the Cowdray Engravings portraying the King's visit to Portsmouth, July 19, 1545

103 Gustavus Adolphus and the Hakkapeliitas at the Battle of Breitenfeld between 1631 and 1677.

104 Louis XIV crossing the Pont Neuf in Paris in a carriage in front of the statue of his grandfather Henry IV. "March of the King accompanied by his guards passing over the Pont-Neuf and going to the Palace" painting by Adam Frans van der Meulen.

105 A mid-19th century painting by Rosa Bonheur, depicting a French horse fair that includes Percherons.

106 The entire European nobility rode Spanish horses during the Baroque age. By https://www.britishmuseum.org/collection/object/P_1982-U-1444, Public Domain, https://commons.wikimedia.org/w/index.php?curid=90345206

107 ladruby nad Labem - Kladruber horses. https://commons.wikimedia.org/wiki File:Kladruby_nad_Labem,_h%C5%99eb%C4%8D%C3%ADn,klisny_s_h%C5%99%C3%ADbaty.jpg#/media/File:Kladruby_nad_Labem,_hřebčín,_klisny_s_hříbaty.jpg

107a Spanish Riding School in Vienna, 1890. - By Heinrich Lang - Illustrierter Katalog der Münchener Jahresausstellung von Kunstwerken Aller Nationen im königl. Glaspalaste 1890, Ausgabe vom Anfang September, München 1890 (Digitalisat der BSB), Public Domain, https://commons.wikimedia.org/w/index.php?curid=17544903

108 Spanish Riding School, Winter Riding School arena, Vienna, Austria. By sparre - File:Spanische Hofreitschule3, Vienna.jpg (cropped), CC BY-SA 3.0, https://commons.wikimedia.org/w/index.php?curid=28916681

109 Prince Henry's School of Navigation, Artist: Mielatz, Charles Frederick William (Breddin, Germany, 1860 - New York, 1919) Charles Frederick William Mielatz's original etching, "Prince Henry's School of Navigation" is an artist proof impression containing a remarque within the lower left margin. It is printed upon 19th century china paper which has been backed onto board and with large margins as printed and published by Charles Mielatz, in New York in 1896. This impression is signed and dated in the plate and is also signed by Mielatz in pencil under the image. Prince Henry's School of Navigation is a fine, original and impressive historical etching created by the late nineteenth century American etcher, Charles Mielatz. http://www.artoftheprint.com/artistpages/mielatz_charles_frederick_william_princehenrysschoolofnavigation.htm

110 Spanish horse in sling during crossing. Many ships that transported horses had slings to keep horses upright. https://equusmagazine.com/blog-equus/slings-horses-history-hope-equine-support-system-32212/

111 Columbus at the court of Ferdinand and Isabella after his first voyage. Columbus takes leave of Europe, engraving of Theodore, early 17th century.

112 Narragansett Pacer. Illustration from Frank Forester's Horse and Horsemanship of the United States and British Provinces of North America (1857). National Sporting Library & Museum, acquired 1981, the gift of Mrs. William Pyemont. https://nslmblog.wordpress.com/2018/02/13/lost-horse-america/

113 Conestoga Horse, engraving from the Report of the Commissioner of Agriculture for the year 1863, page 175. By unsigned - Report of the Commissioner of Agriculture for the year 1863, U.S. Department of Agriculture 1864, Public Domain, https://commons.wikimedia.org/w/index.php?curid=80119222

114 Conestoga Wagon 1883. By https://commons.wikimedia.org/wiki/User:AdMeskens - Wikimedia Commons, Public Domain, https://commons.wikimedia.org/w/index.php?curid=50604118

115 Statue of Justin Morgan in Vermont (home of the Morgan horse) Dedicated in 1921 at UVM. https://www.vtattractions.org/uvm-morgan-horse-farm/

116 The British evacuate Boston, March 17, 1776.. J. Godfrey after painting by Michael Angelo Wageman.

117 Slowly the continent spanning nation was forming. By United States federal government (en:User:Black and White converted it from JPEG to PNG and retouched it) - National Atlas of the United States [1], Public Domain, https://commons.wikimedia.org/w/index.php?curid=1178618

118 The original McCormick Reaper as invented in 1831. McCormick's invention gave the farmer an extra power surce – the horse. https://www.britannica.com/biography/Cyrus-McCormick

119 Horses and mules were used to get supplies to the towns in large freight wagons. By Miscellaneous Items in High Demand, PPOC, Library of Congress - Library of CongressCatalog: https://lccn.loc.gov/2013647269Image download: https://cdn.loc.gov/master/pnp/cph/3a40000/3a40000/3a40600/3a40651u.tifOriginal url: https://www.loc.gov/pictures/item/2013647269/, Public Domain, https://commons.wikimedia.org/w/index.php?curid=67988640

120 Pony Express. https://www.archives.gov/historical-docs/todays-doc/index.html?dod-date=403

121 Union army wagon train halted and guarded from Confederate cavalry near Brandy Station, VA, in May 1863. http://www.thomaslegion.net/americancivilwar/totalcivilwarhorseskilled.html

122 The Leister farm right after the battle. https://gettysburg.stonesentinels.com/battlefield-farms/leister-farm-meades-headquarters/

123 Map of the Detroit United Railway including the Detroit & Port Huron Shore Line. https://maps.lib.utexas.edu/maps/mcgraw_electric.html?p=print[-Michigan, Ohio, Ontario] "Map of the Detroit United Railway including the Detroit & Port Huron Shore Line Ry." (Rapid Railway 186 System); Detroit, Monroe & Tol. Short Line Ry.; Detroit, Jackson &
Chicago Ry.; and the Sandwich, Windsor &Amherstburg Ry."

124 Draft horse breeding programs in Canada flourished during the late 19th and early 20th centuries in response to the agricultural sector's demand for more horsepower. Photo courtesy of the Provincial Archives of Alberta. https://www.dailypress.com/history/dp-nws-world-war-i-war-horses-1-20141129-story.html

125 To accommodate the rapidly increasing needs of the army, there were eventually 33 auxiliary remount depots established, plus two animal embarkation depots including Newport News, RH. https://www.worldwar1centennial.org/index.php/brookeusa-training-forwar/4548-brooke-usa-the-remountservice.html

126 Fifth Avenue in New York City on Easter Sunday in 1900. By U.S. Bureau of Public Roads. Photographer unknown. - National Archives and Records Administration, Records of the Bureau of Public Roads. Image 30-N-18827, from https://www.archives.gov/exhibits/picturing_the_century/newcent/newcent_img1.html Also found as #101 at https://www.archives.gov/research/american-cities/

127 Fifth Avenue, Easter Sunday 1913. By U.S. Bureau of Public Roads.

128 From Okanagan School of Natural Hoof Care. https://www.irongateequine.com/education/laminitis

129 Navicular Anatomy. From the Collection of Gloria Austin.

130 The Stages of Equine Skeletal Development. Created by Naomi Tavian, @equinaomi

131 Ligaments and Tendons of the leg by Dr. Robin Peterson/The horse. Horse Anatomy

Pictures-Think Like a Horse-Rick Gore Horsemanship. A complete site about horses, their behavior, riding and training horses with understanding and knowledge and the anatomy of horses. http://thinklikeahorse.org/index-5.html

132 Ligaments and muscles of the horse. Image by: Gillian Higgins. http://curlyhorsecountry.com/horseanatomy.htm and https://www.horsesinsideout.com/home

133 Conformation of the horse. https://extension.umn.edu/horse-care-and-management/conformation-horse#pasterns-1159012)

134 Horse Gaits by illustrator Helga Jaunegg

135 Kristi Wysocki shows where a horse's Center of Balance is on Lynn McEnespy's 6-year-old Hanoverian gelding, Wredford.

136 Gabor Nicholas Foltenyi, born in Hungary in 1922, received his first horse at age 10. https://horsenetwork.com/2021/09/halloffamethursday-gabor-foltenyi/

137 Dressage versus jumper conformation https://www.behindthebitblog.com/2008/06/dressage-versus-jumper-conformation.html

137a PRE STALLION • Wetter (Hessen), Germany. Extreme beautyful PRE Stallion. Ridden in the 3 Gaites. Full ANCCE papers with best Pedigree. Vet check with 18 X-Rays. Kathrin Langpaap-Kupfer https://www.horsescout.com/horses-for-sale/profile/4986

138 Dressage Hind End Conformation. https://www.behindthebitblog.com/2008/06/dressage-versus-jumper-conformation.html

139 Overall Conformation for Dressage . From Nancy Kerson's mustang research.

140 Collection. By Renate Blank - Klaus Schöneich Zentrum für Anatomisch richtiges Reiten® & Schiefen-Therapie®, CC BY-SA 2.5, https://commons.wikimedia.org/w/index.php?curid=1256354

141 Tomb of Amenemopet called Tjanefe. Fragment of a limestone tomb-painting representing the assessment of crops, for the purposes of tax, on Nebamun's estate, five vertical registers of hieroglyphs survive; the rest of the fragment is divided into two registers, with a horse-drawn chariot above and cart drawn by onagars beneath. 1350BC (circa), 18th Egyptian dynasty. Excavated/Findspot: Tomb of Nebamun (Thebes) Africa: Egypt: Upper Egypt: Tomb of Nebamun (Thebes) https://www.britishmuseum.org/collection/object/Y_EA37982

142 The Sling Muscles and Self-Carriage. https://www.swannequineosteo.com/blog/2017/12/5/equine-biomechanics-research-the-significance-of-a-horses-chest-sling-muscles

143 The definitive horse for racing is the Thoroughbred. Quarter Horses and Arabians are also used for racing but at venues for their specific breed; they do not compete against Thoroughbreds. Standardbreds are used for harness racing. The Tony Leonard Collection (@the_tony_leonard_collection) on Instagram: "Swaps conformation!

144 Inglis Premier Superhero Black Caviar (Bel Esprit x Helsinge) as a yearling at the 2008 Inglis Melbourne Premier Yearling Sale where she was purchased by trainer Peter Moody for $210,000 from the draft of Swettenham Stud as agent for Gilgai Farm. https://www.facebook.com/InglisPremier/

144a American Standardbred - Mach Three (a Pacer), A son of Matts Scooter out of All Included, Mach Three was owned by the Muscara Racing Trust of Ivyland, Pennsylvania. The late Joe Muscara Sr. of Huntingdon Valley, Pennsylvania purchased the pacer in May of Mach Three's sophomore season from Linda Magid of Cambridge, Ont., the widow of the pacer's breeder, Karl Magid. Photo by Dave Landry. https://standardbredcanada.ca/news/1-20-17/mach-three-euthanized-new-zealand.html

145 Standardbred racehorses are the product of interbreeding of thoroughbred racehorses, various pacer breeds and Norfolk Trotters.. Photo by Viivi Huuskonen, https://www.flickr.com/photos/viivihuuskonen/7996657375/

146 Alfred Hanover, a Pacer Standard bred in race where he placed 2nd with Ron Burk. Northfield, Ohio, July 2022.

147 Seaman - a long distance runner. Photo by Carlos David - David Racing LLC.

147a Picture 1 - Arab Conformation of Farley, Dr. Mel Blog https://melnewton.com/2015/the-way-i-see-it/

147b Picture 2 - Arab Conformation of Farley, Dr. Mel Blog https://melnewton.com/2015/the-way-i-see-it/

148 Saddle Seat horse. 2000 Registered American Saddlebred gelding, named Flash. Sorrel with flaxen mane and tail, blaze and three white socks. 15.3 hands. Photos above taken June of 2015, with the great help of my new friends, Catherine & Linda! https://www.saddlebred-horses.com/horses-sold.html

149 Conformation of the American Saddlebred. https://equinehusbandry.ces.ncsu.edu/wp-content/uploads/2015/02/Conformation-of-the-American-Saddlebred.pdf?fwd=no

150 Conformation for Western Performance - https://www.horsetrainingvideos.com/free-horse-training.htm

151 Barrel Racing. Spencerville Stampede, July 2014. By cjuneau - IMG_5230-1, CC BY 2.0, https://commons.wikimedia.org/w/index.php?curid=37286512

152 Roping. Robert Wood, "About Roping, the Rodeo Event." Topend Sports Website, February 2016, https://www.topendsports.com/sport/list/rodeo-roping.htm, Accessed 19 August 2022. https://www.topendsports.com/sport/list/rodeo-roping.htm

153 Reining. Matt Mills, the 2015 $25,000 Adequan/USEF Open Reining National Reserve Champion, riding Freckles Got AShiner (Waltenberry) https://www.usef.org/media/press-releases/2017-usef-reining-national-championships-set-to

154 Cutting. https://www.americanfarriers.com/articles/212-understanding-the-cutting-horses-job?v=preview

155 Arabians, Morgans, Tennessee Walkers, Rocky Mountain Horse, Draft crosses and Mules are breeds often used for trail and packing. Tevis Cup Ride by Kelsey Brown.

156 Appaloosa Horses and Pony of Americas. https://montanatrailhorse.com/best-trail-horses/

157 Pack Horse and Mule with Rifle/Bow Scabbard. https://www.gunsamerica.com/digest/5-tips-for-packing-gear-with-horses-mules/

158 Draft-Cross Horses. https://montanatrailhorse.com/best-trail-horses/

159 Hayden, a Cey seven-year-old stallion, was named Supreme Grand Champion Clyde at the Calgary Stampede Heavy Horse Show, beating out both the previous Western Canadian champion and the Eastern champion stud who had won at the Royal Agricultural Winter Fair in Toronto., Ont., last fall. Ken Cey of Scott, along with sons Derek and Kent and their families, own 60 head of purebred black Clydesdales and expect their herd to produce 27 new foals in the spring of 2016. https://www.sasktoday.ca/north/local-news/the-cey-clydesdales-of-scott-gaining-worldwide-recognition-4079604

160 The Belgian Draft Horse is a photograph by JC Findley which was uploaded on April 12th, 2018. https://fineartamerica.com/featured/the-belgian-draft-horse-jc-findley.html

161 F.P. Icepick, Percheron Stallion. http://www.utopiapercherons.com/

162 Jumping. Horse Know It All, Baden Württemberg, Pinterest, The Chronicle of the Horse / Lisa Slade. https://www.globetrotting.com.au/horse-breed-trakehner-2/

163 Spanish Dressage Horses - https://spanish-dressagehorses.com/?page_id=616&lang=en

164 Standardbred trotter stallion, Art Major. https://www.bluechipfarms.com/

165 Suffolk Punch, a heavy draft horse from England, always chestnut in color. The breed almost died out in the mid to late 20th century as work horses were not required, but rare breed registries are working to increase its very low numbers. https://www.thesuffolkpunchtrust.co.uk/

166 We are a family company and through generations we have been dedicated to the world-wide supply of top quality Shire and Clydesdale Horses. https://www.shiresandclydesdales.com/

167 Trail/Packing - "Triumph" a British Army pack-horse in 1914, epitomises the perfect type of pack-horse. http://www.thelongridersguild.com/stories/pack-horse.htm

168 https://memes.com/template/1033

169 Colors and Markings. www.venomxbaby.deviantart.com

170 Horse Whorls. Swirlology, The Study of Hair Swirls or Whorls in Horses by Charlotte Cannon. https://img1.wsimg.com/blobby/go/ad820a14-9618-4fa4-b564-3128cb783a8d/downloads/2018%20Swirlology%20pdf.pdf?ver=1626959297683

171 Tyson and Hark, in a snowy paddock. Photo by Mary Chris Foxworthy.